MAKING BIG WORDS

Multilevel, Hands-on Phonics and Spelling Activities

by
Patricia M. Cunningham
and
Dorothy P. Hall

Good Apple

Dedication

Dedicated to Connie Prevatte—an intermediate- and middle-school teacher who is now consulting with teachers and helping them achieve balanced reading programs in which children read and write and enjoy learning about how words work.

Editor
Donna Garzinsky

Designer
Ruth Otey
Deborah Walkoczy

Cover Design
Peter Van Ryzin
Bernadette Hruby

Cover Photographs
John Paul Endress

GOOD APPLE
A Division of Frank Schaffer Publications
23740 Hawthorne Blvd.
Torrance, CA 90505

CONTENTS

Introduction	4
Theory and Research	5
References	8
Planning and Teaching a Lesson	9
Planning Your Own Lessons	15
Tips for Successful Lessons	16
More Tips	17
Phonics and Spelling Patterns	17
About These Lessons	17
Student Letter Holders	17
Letter Strips	17
Curriculum Connections	18
Letter to Families	20
Lessons Index	21
Lessons	44
Patterns Index	194
Prefixes, Suffixes, and Endings	194
Digraphs and Consonants	196
Homophones	197
Rimes and Spelling Patterns	199
Compound Words	205
Letter Strips Reproducibles	208

INTRODUCTION

Making More Big Words follows in the footsteps of its predecessor, *Making Big Words*. The lessons in *Making More Big Words* have been used by teachers who've chosen and adapted the lessons to suit the needs of their classes. The lessons begin on page 44 and are arranged alphabetically by the big word that ends the lesson. They can be used in any order (see Lessons Index, on p. 21). A Patterns Index of prefixes, suffixes, and endings; digraphs and consonants; homophones; rimes and spelling patterns; and compound words provides the letter patterns that can be sorted for each big word (see p. 194). Some teachers find this index useful for identifying several *Making More Big Words* lessons with particular patterns that can be taught in a row to provide more practice for students.

In addition to the lessons, lessons index, and patterns index, *Making More Big Words* contains reproducible letter strips for each lesson (p. 208) and a sample letter to send home to families (p. 20). (See p. 17 for more information on the letter strips.) Some teachers duplicate enough letter strips so that each student can take home an uncut strip of the lesson's letters. Students can't wait to take the strips home and say, "I bet you don't know the big word that can be made when you use all these letters!" At home they cut the strips into letters and let someone—parent, brother, sister, grand-mother—try to make the big word. They then proudly demonstrate words they can remember making and how they sorted these words into patterns.

Information on the theory and research behind *Making More Big Words* is included on page 5. For tips on teaching a lesson, see Planning and Teaching a Lesson (p. 9), Tips for Successful Lessons (p. 16), and About These Lessons (p. 17). For help in selecting lessons that focus on particular letter patterns, see Phonics and Spelling Patterns (p. 17). For ideas on creating your own *Making More Big Words* lessons, see Planning Your Own Lessons (p. 15). For suggestions on integrating lessons with other class curricula, see Curriculum Connections, on page 18.

Making More Big Words is a manipulative, multilevel activity that both teachers and students enjoy. As students make and sort words, they increase their word knowledge, discover patterns, and become more able readers and writers.

Making More Big Words is an activity in which students are individually given some letters, and they use the letters to make words. During the 15–20 minute activity, students make approximately 15–20 words, beginning with short words and continuing with bigger words until the final word is made. This word always includes all the letters students have to use in that lesson. Students are usually eager to figure out what word can be made from all the letters.

Making More Big Words is an active, hands-on, manipulative activity in which students discover letter-sound relationships and learn how to look for patterns in words. They also learn that changing just one letter or even just the sequence of letters changes the whole word (Cunningham, 1991; Cunningham and Cunningham, 1992).

After making the words, the students help the teacher sort the words for patterns. They may pull out all the words that begin alike or that have a particular spelling pattern or vowel sound. They also sort for endings, prefixes and suffixes, homophones (*close; clothes*), and compound words.

Making More Big Words is a multilevel activity because, within one instructional format, there are endless possibilities for discovering how our alphabetic system works. By beginning every *Making More Big Words* activity with some short easy words and ending with a big word that uses all the letters, the lessons provide practice for the slowest learners and challenge for all. It is a quick, every-pupil response, manipulative activity that actively involves all students.

Spelling-pattern and word-family instruction has a long history in American reading instruction. Currently, research is converging from several areas that supports the long-standing practice of word family/phonogram/spelling pattern instruction. The research of Treiman (1985) suggests that both children and adults find it much easier to divide syllables into their onsets (all the letters before a vowel) and rimes (a vowel and letters that follow) than into any other units. Thus *Sam* is more easily divided into *S - am* than into *Sa - m* or *S-a-m*. It is easier and quicker for people to change *Sam* to *ham* and *jam* than it is to change *Sam* to *sat* and *sad*. In fact, Treiman concludes that the division of words into onset and rime is a "psychological reality." Wylie and Durrell (1970) listed 37 phonograms that could be found in almost 500 primary-grade words. These high-utility phonograms are

> *ack; ail; ain; ake; ale; ame; an; ank; ap; ash; at; ate; aw; ay; eat; ell; est; ice; ick; ide; ight; ill; in; ine; ing; ink; ip; it; ock; oke; op; ore; ot; uck; ug; ump; unk*

Another area of research supporting spelling patterns is that conducted on decoding by analogy (Goswami & Bryant, 1990). This research suggests that once students have some words that they can read and spell, they use these known words to figure out unknown words. A reader confronting the infrequent word *flounce* for the first time might access the known words *ounce* and *pounce* and then use these words to generate a probable pronunciation for *flounce.*

Brain research provides a different sort of support for word family instruction. Current theory suggests that the brain is a pattern detector, not a rule applier, and that decoding a word occurs when the brain recognizes a familiar spelling pattern or, if the pattern itself is not familiar, searches through its store of words with similar patterns (Adams, 1990). To decode the unfamiliar word, *knob,* for example, the child who knew many words that began with *kn* would immediately assign to the *kn* the "*n*" sound. The initial *kn* would be stored in the brain as a spelling pattern. If the child only knew a few other words with *kn* and hadn't read these words very often, that child would probably not have *kn* as a known spelling pattern and thus would have to do a quick search for known words that began with *kn.* If the child found the words *know* and *knew* and then tried this same sound on the unknown word *knob,* the child would have used the analogy strategy. Likewise, the child might know the pronunciation for *ob* because of having correctly read so many words containing the *ob* spelling pattern or might have had to access some words with *ob* to use them to come up with the pronunciation. The child who had no stored spelling patterns for *kn* or *ob* and no known words to access and compare to would be unlikely to successfully pronounce the unknown word *knob.*

Big words have some additional patterns beyond the common one-syllable spelling patterns. The patterns in big words include prefixes and suffixes, which give semantic clues about meanings for words in addition to serving as pronunciation chunks. Recognizing the prefix *mis-* in words like *misread* and *mistreat* helps students access both meaning and pronunciation. In *Mississippi* and *mistletoe,* the *mis-* still helps with pronunciation but not with meaning. Suffixes such as *-tion* and *-al* affect the pronunciation of words and change where in the sentence the words can be used. In English many big words are just little words with added prefixes and suffixes. When you *act* in a certain way, you perform an *action*. Sometimes our *action* provokes a *reaction*. People who *overreact* are called *reactionaries*.

To determine how good readers decode and spell big words, we must consider what we know about how the brain functions and specifically how big words are analyzed and divided. Decades of research by Mewhort and colleagues (summarized in Mewhort and Campbell, 1981, and in Adams, 1990) demonstrate that good readers "chunk," or divide big words into manageable units. They do this based on the brain's incredible knowledge of which letters usually go together in words. If you did not recognize the word *midnight* in print, you would divide it as you saw it, between the *d* and the *n*. For the word *Madrid*, however, you would divide after the *a*, leaving the *dr* together. Interletter frequency theory explains this neatly by pointing out that the letters *dr* often occur together in syllables in words you know (*drop, dry, Dracula*). Words with the letters *dn* in the same syllable are almost nonexistent. (This also explains why beginners might pronounce *f-a-t-h-e-r* as "fat her," but children who have some words from which the brain can generate interletter frequencies will leave the *th* together and pronounce "*father.*")

Psychological theory suggests that the brain functions as a pattern detector. Successfully decoding a word occurs when the brain recognizes a familiar spelling pattern or, if the pattern itself is not familiar, searches through its store of words with similar patterns. To find patterns in big words, the brain "chunks" the word not based on rules but on its incredible knowledge of interletter frequencies. Once big words are chunked, readers use patterns from known big words to decode the unfamiliar word. In order to use patterns from known words, readers must have a store of multisyllabic words that they can read and spell.

If you ask students what they think of *Making More Big Words*, they will probably answer, "It's fun!" From the moment that students get their letters, they begin moving the letters around and making whatever words they can. They are particularly eager to figure out the word that can be made with all the letters. Once students begin making the words the teacher asks them to make, the activity is fast-paced and keeps the students involved. They also enjoy sorting the words. Students put words together in groups that have the same spelling pattern, prefix, suffix or other pattern, and then other students have to guess why they put those particular words together. *Making More Big Words* lessons involve the students in looking at words and manipulating words. Through these activities they learn to recognize and spell many big words, and they discover the patterns that allow them to decode and spell new big words.

REFERENCES

Adams, M. J. *Beginning to Read: Thinking and Learning About Print.* MIT Press, Cambridge, MA, 1990.

Cunningham, P. M. *Phonics They Use: Words for Reading and Writing.* HarperCollins, New York, 1991.

Cunningham, P. M. and J. W. Cunningham. "Making Words: Enhancing the Invented Spelling-Decoding Connection." *The Reading Teacher,* 46, 106–115, 1992.

Goswami, U. and P. Bryant. *Phonological Skills and Learning to Read.* Erlbaum Associates, East Sussex, U.K., 1990.

Henderson, E. H. *Teaching Spelling* (2nd ed.). Houghton Mifflin, Boston, 1990.

Treiman, R. "Onsets and Rimes as Units of Spoken Syllables: Evidence From Children." *Journal of Experimental Child Psychology,* 39, 161–181, 1985.

Wylie, R. E. and D. D. Durrell. "Teaching Vowels Through Phonograms." *Elementary English,* 47, 787–791, 1970.

▪ Planning the Lesson ▪

The teacher has decided that *magazines* is the word that will end the lesson. She has pulled out the large letter cards for *magazines*. Here, she is brainstorming lots of words that can be made from the letters in *magazines*.

The teacher has decided which of the many words that could be made will provide a multilevel lesson and will give patterns to sort for. She writes these words on large index cards.

She puts these index cards in a small brown envelope. On the outside of the envelope, she writes the words in the order the students will make them, the patterns she will have them sort for, and the transfer words.

Here is the envelope with the words to be made and the letter strips. Each strip has the printed letters *a a e i g m n s z,* vowels then consonants in alphabetical order so as not to give away what the big word is.

Students are given strips containing the letters of the big word. The children cut the strips into individual letters. They then have two minutes to figure out all the words they can make from these letters before making the words the teacher has decided they should make.

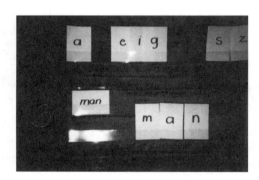

The teacher writes a 3 on the board and says,
    "The first word I want you to make has just three letters. Take three letters and make the word *man*."

A student who has made the word *man* correctly comes and makes it with the pocket-chart letters.
    "Good, *m-a-n* spells *man*. Everyone check *man* and we are ready to make another word."

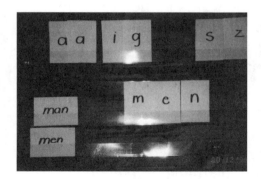

The teacher places the index card for *man* in the pocket chart. She tells them to change one letter and spell the word *men*.

The children continue to make three-letter words as directed by the teacher. When the word is made with the pocket-chart letters, the teacher reminds students to fix their word if it is not correct and then places the index card with that word in the pocket chart. Here is the pocket chart with the three-letter words.

man	zag
men	zig
gem	age
nag	

The teacher writes a 4 on the board and asks the children to add one letter to *age* and change *age* to *sage*.

"Sage is a spice used in cooking and also a word for a very wise person."

This girl is making the word *sage* with big letters.

Students continue to spell four-letter words until the pocket chart looks like this.

man	sage
men	zing
gem	sing
nag	sign
zag	size
zig	gaze
age	maze

The teacher writes a 5 on the board and asks students to add a letter to *maze* to spell *amaze*. Students spell another five-letter word, *image*. Next they leave the *a-g-e* but change the first part to spell the six-letter word *manage*. The teacher writes a 7 on the board and asks them to use just seven letters to spell *amazing*. (This puzzles the children who would like to leave the *e* on the end of *amaze* and add *-ing*, but they figure it out!) Next the teacher asks them to take a stab at a hard-to-spell seven-letter word, *amnesia*.

The teacher tells the students that every *Making More Big Words* lesson ends with a word that uses all the letters.
"Move your letters around and see if you can make a word that uses all the letters."

The students are given one minute to see if anyone can come up with the word.

If anyone makes the word, the teacher sends that student to the pocket chart to make the word. If not, the teacher tells students that the word is *magazines* and has them make it.

The teacher and children are now going to sort the words for patterns. First the teacher has children pull out all the words with a *g* in them and then sort these *g* words according to the two sounds for *g*, putting *sign* by itself because the *g* in *sign* has no sound.

gem	nag	sign
age	zag	
sage	zig	
image	zing	
manage	sing	
	gaze	
	magazines	

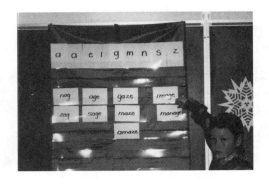

The second sort is for words that end in *-ag, -age* or *-aze*. Once sorted out and pronounced, the *a-g-e* words are then subdivided according to the pronunciation.

nag	age	gaze	image
zag	sage	maze	manage
		amaze	

When the words are lined up according to spelling patterns and rhymes, the teacher says

"When you are reading, you will see lots of words that end in these spelling patterns, and you can figure them out if you think about how words with the same spelling pattern usually rhyme. What if you were reading and came to these words?"

The teacher writes the words *glaze* and *cage* on index cards without pronouncing them. Students put these words under the rhyming words and then use the rhyming words to figure them out.

"Thinking of a rhyming word can help you when you are writing, too. What if you were writing and needed to figure out how to spell *bag* or *baggage*?"

The children decide that *bag* rhymes with *nag* and *zag*. The teacher writes *bag* on an index card and places it under *nag* and *zag*. The word *baggage* is spelled and then placed under *image* and *manage*.

nag	age	gaze	image
zag	sage	maze	manage
bag	cage	amaze	baggage
		blaze	

PLANNING YOUR OWN LESSONS

Once you get started *Making More Big Words*, you will find that many of the words that tie into your content are not included in our lessons. It's fun and easy to plan lessons of your own. Here are the steps we went through to plan our lessons.

1. Decide what the final word in the lesson will be. In choosing this word, consider student interest, what curriculum tie-ins you can make, and what patterns you can draw student's attention to through the word sorting at the end of the lesson.

2. Make a list of words that can be made from the letters of the final word.

3. From all the words you listed, pick approximately 15–20 words that include

   a. Words that you can sort for the pattern(s) you want to emphasize

   b. Little words and big words so that the lesson is multilevel

   c. Words that can be made with the same letters in different places (*quiet/quite*) so that children are reminded that when spelling words, the order of the letters is crucial

   d. Homophones and compound words

   e. Words that most of the students have in their listening vocabularies

4. Write all the words on index cards and order them from smallest to largest.

5. Order them further so that you can emphasize letter patterns and how changing the position of the letters or changing or adding just one letter results in a different word.

6. Store the cards in an envelope. Write on the envelope the words in order, the patterns you will sort for, and some transfer words that can be spelled based on these patterns.

TIPS FOR SUCCESSFUL LESSONS

Many teachers have found the following tips helpful.

1. Pace your lesson quickly. If a lesson moves too slowly, students get bored! Don't wait for all students to make each word before sending someone to the pocket chart.

2. Adapt the lesson to your class. Leave out words that are too difficult or that your students have never heard of.

3. Have students say each word—not just listen for the word—before making it. Students need to hear themselves making the sounds if they are going to transfer this ability to spelling words as they write.

4. Make sure you leave time to sort and transfer. Some students need to be explicitly taught how making words helps them read and spell. If you are keeping a brisk pace and you run out of time to sort and transfer, make fewer words.

5. Remember that *Making More Big Words* is a multilevel activity. Send your strugglers to the pocket chart to show how to make the easier words and your word wizards to show how to make the more complex words.

6. Give students more guidance in making and sorting words early in the year and then phase out some of that guidance.

    For example, early in the year, say
       "Change the first letter to change *mash* to *cash*."
    Later, say
       "Change just one letter to change *mash* to *cash*."
    When sorting early in the year, say
       "Who can find the words that rhyme with *ash*?"
    Later, say
       "Who can come and sort out the rhyming words?"

7. Let students take their letters home to make more words and see who at home can figure out the big word!

8. Many teacher workrooms have a communal box filled with brown *Making More Big Words* envelopes. When a teacher finishes a lesson, it is added to the box.

9. Most lessons are used only once by each teacher, but sometimes teachers use the same lesson again several months later, when it fits in with something else they are doing.

▪ Phonics and Spelling Patterns ▪

Sometimes, teachers do a lesson because children need work with the patterns sorted for in that lesson. Use the patterns index on page 194 to find words containing the following patterns.

    prefixes, suffixes, endings

    homophones

    digraphs, consonants

    rimes, spelling patterns

    compound words

▪ About These Lessons ▪

The slash (/) indicates that the next word can be made by changing the order of the letters. Words with an asterisk (*) are harder to spell or less apt to be in students' listening vocabularies and may be omitted to make the lesson easier or shorter. Remember that including some harder words makes your lesson multilevel.

▪ Student Letter Holders ▪

You may wish to provide simple letter holders for students to use. Inexpensive holders can be easily fashioned from self-stick notes.

- For each letter holder, use two 5 in. by 3 in. (12.7 cm X 7.6 cm) self-stick notes. Place the two notes next to each other, sticky side face down. Match the sides up, then tape the sides of the two notes together. Turn the taped notes over.

- Students can position and reposition letters on the sticky portion of the self-stick notes for a number of lessons before new holders will be needed.

- Holders can also be stored folded (with the sticky sides facing in or out) in student folders or binders.

▪ Letter Strips ▪

The reproducible letter strips, found on pages 208–224, are arranged in three groups: letter strips for words needing no upper-case letters (pp. 208–217), blank letter strips to use in creating your own lessons (p. 218), and letter strips for words that use lowercase and uppercase letters (pp. 219–224). The last group provides lowercase letters on one page and uppercase letters on the next page. Reproduce as is, letting students choose among the letters on the two strips, or create two-sided letters by positioning related pages on the photocopier so that the uppercase and lowercase letter blocks line up.

CURRICULUM CONNECTIONS

To be effective, phonics and spelling instruction should be tied as closely as possible to what children are reading and learning about. In selecting the word that ends the lesson, we have included below many words that teachers use as part of their themes or units.

Health, Nutrition, Safety
- Accidents
- Antibiotics
- Carelessness
- Cauliflower
- Cholesterol
- Cleanliness
- Ingredients
- Pneumonia
- Relaxation
- Toothbrushes
- Undernourished
- Vaccination
- Vegetarians

Reading, Literature
- Biography
- Bookstore
- Characters
- Communication
- Comprehension
- Libraries
- Literature
- Magazines
- Mysteries
- Newspapers
- Vocabulary

Language, Describing Words
- Adventurous
- Beautiful
- Enthusiastic
- Exhausting
- Fashionable
- Frightening
- Handicapped
- Kindhearted
- Misunderstood
- Responsible
- Sensational
- Spectacular
- Unconscious
- Unfortunate
- Unsatisfactory
- Unsuccessful

Careers, Occupations
- Astronauts
- Bullfighter
- Carpenters
- Electricians
- Inspectors
- Interviews
- Lumberjacks
- Psychologist
- Reporters
- Veterinarian

Celebrations, Holidays
- Anniversary
- Birthdays
- Celebrating
- Congratulations
- Decorations
- Festivals
- Invitations
- Poinsettias
- Refreshments

Weather
- Barometers
- Blizzards
- Destruction
- Evaporation
- Meteorologists
- Precipitation
- Snowstorm
- Unpredictable
- Volcanoes

Environment
- Endangered
- Environment
- Greenhouse
- Photosynthesis
- Pollutants
- Scientists
- Telescopes
- Wilderness

Animals
Alligators
Amphibians
Blackbirds
Carnivores
Caterpillars
Centipedes
Crocodiles
Dinosaurs
Ducklings
Hibernation
Hippopotamus
Mockingbirds
Mosquitoes
Rattlesnakes
Rhinoceros

Geography
Australia
Baltimore
Connecticut
Continent
Countries
Geography
Milwaukee
Minnesota
Philadelphia
Pittsburgh

Community, Family
Community
Grandchildren
Grandfathers
Grandmothers
Immigrants
Neighborhood
Relatives
Traditions

Government
Americans
Amendments
Candidates
Democracy
Elections
Governments
Independence
Presidents
Unemployment

Math
Calculators
Estimating
Fractions
Kilometers
Mathematics
Measuring
Millimeters
Multiplying
Perpendicular
Rectangles
Subtracting
Thousands
Triangles

Sports
Badminton
Breakthroughs
Champions
Cheerleaders
Footballs
Gymnastics
Interception
Interference
Outfielders
Scoreboard
Semifinals
Skateboarding
Teammates
Tournaments
Underdogs
Volleyballs

Dear FAMILIES

Making More Big Words is an important hands-on activity that students work on in class. Each day, students "learn by doing" to make words. As students manipulate the given letters, they discover more about letter-sound relationships, and as they look for patterns in words, they see how these letter-sound relationships work in words. These two activities help students read and spell even more words! Children enjoy these lessons, but more importantly these skills increase their word knowledge, which will help them become even better students and readers in the future.

When your child brings home his or her letter strip, have the child cut the letter strip apart into the individual letters. Next, let your child see how many words he or she can make. Finally, the child takes some of the words and puts them into groups (your child knows what to do). You may want to work together with your child or just see the finished list and how the words were sorted. Working with words can be fun as well as educational!

Sincerely,

_____

Your child's teacher

20

LESSONS INDEX

The following lessons are in alphabetical order.

1. **accidents** *ance end ie tide/tied lie*   44
    end and ant die tie tied/tide/diet/edit send tend
    dance *stance *antics *scenic insect instead candies
    distance accidents

2. **adventurous** *ous end ound*   45
    end send tend tour trend sound round around
    nature detour starve reason treason astound
    nervous *arduous *ravenous adventurous

3. **alligators** *all ill oll*   46
    go ago all ill gill tall toll also riot/*trio *ratio
    atlas *alias troll grill still girls solar stroll sailor
    gorillas alligators

4. **amendments** *ed* (spelling changes) *an en eat*   47
    meat-meet
    man men ten tan Stan seat neat meat meet
    name named *dense *tense tease teased/seated
    *senate tanned manned amendments

5. **Americans** *ace eam* Word relatives: *anemia,*   48
    anemic . . .
    arm ace race mace cream mania maniac
    *anemia *anemic camera scream armies racism
    marina marines/remains *arsenic America *amnesia
    *amnesiac Americans

6. **amphibians** *am ap ash ip*   49
    arm Sam ham has/ash map nap sap sip ship
    snip snap bash mash smash *banish *mishap
    amphibians

7. **anniversary** *y-ies ain ane* (two spellings, one   50
    pronunciation) *rain-rein vain-vane-vein a-area, arena,*
    arise, arisen, arrive
    rain-rein vein-vain-vane sane very-vary navy
    area earn *yearn river arena arise *arisen arrive
    insane navies varies *ravine anniversary

8. **antibiotics** *tion ic oat oast roast picnic*   51
fiction friction
act ant ants boat coat coats/coast boast toast
bacon basic tonic sonic attic static action station
*Titanic *botanist antibiotics

9. **astronauts** *art *ort our out ut ust un*   52
sun-son shout short scour outsmart
art out nut rut run sun son our sour sort
tart rust stun stunt start trust/strut trout *stout
*snout *snort astronauts

10. **Australia** *at ar ail it ir Asia, Austria, Australia*   53
fail brat jar quit
sir sit sat rat/tar star stir slit/list Asia sail tail
rail trail/trial *atlas *ultra Austria Australia

11. **badminton** *ad at it ind words ending in mb*   54
grind glad split flat
it bit bat mat mad bad mind bind into
*atom lamb tomb omit *baton nomad
admit bandit nation *dominant badminton

12. **Baltimore** *ore oil ile words ending in mb smile*   55
spoil chore shore
oil ore tore bore more/Rome mile tile lamb
limb tomb toil boil broil trail/trial tribe tribal
*timber *limber *mobile Baltimore

13. **barometers** *re art east oast be-bee roam-Rome*   56
least toast chart restart
be bee art Bart roam Rome tomb east beast
boast roast smart steam stream remote rebate
resort *arrest *armrest barometers

14. **beautiful** *at ate ale ail* (one pronunciation, two   57
spellings) *elt bale-bail tail-tale melt state*
mail male
at fat eat/ate bat bet belt felt fail blue/lube
tube fate late/tale tail bail bale/able table
fable *built beautiful

15. **biography** *ph y* (two pronunciations) *ay oy sky*   58
stray joy shy
by pry pro boa Roy boy bay bray pray gray
grab *orgy ahoy hair hairy graph *phobia
biography

16. birthdays *y* (two pronunciations) *ay   irt   ird   squirt   flirt   flirty   spray*   59
day shy try tray bird dirt yard tidy hair hairy
dairy/diary daisy dirty *tardy third shirt stray
*radish birthdays

17. blackbirds *ark   ack   ick   id   stack   stick   spark   slid*   60
ask kid skid slid bald said risk bark dark lark
lack rack back lick sick slick slack black brick
brisk blackbirds

18. blizzards *ad   id   ab   aid   paid   afraid   skid   crab*   61
bad sad lad lid bid rid lab labs/slab drab Brad
bird bald raid braid/*rabid *dials *lizard blizzards

19. bookstore *ook   oot   oost   oke   ore   or-ore   shoot*   62
shore   joke   cookbook
or ore sore tore took book boot root roost
boost brook store broke stoke stroke robots
retook booster bookstore

20. breakthroughs *ake   eak* (two pronunciations) *age*   63
(two pronunciations) *ough   ought   ue   brake-break
steak-stake   horse-hoarse* Word relatives: *store, storage;
use, usage . . . thought   glue   leak   lake*
use/sue hue age rage bake beak teak true
argue rough tough ought stage usage store
short brake/break steak/stake horse hoarse
streak bought sought though through brought
hostage storage outrage outbreak shortage
surrogate breakthroughs

21. bullfighter *er   ell   ill   ull   ight* Word relatives: *fill,*   64
refill . . . pull   spill   shell   lighter
big beg bug bull full fill fell bell bill fight
light right bright fright flight *thrill refill
*bullet fighter bullfighter

22. calculators *al   all   oll   mall   poll   scroll   small*   65
call tall toll roll also clot clout coral stall
atlas court troll stroll rascal *actual *casual
cactus crocus coastal *callous calculators

23. candidates *c   an   ance   ed   *ead* (two spellings, one   66
pronunciation) *ide   tide-tied* Word relatives: *sad, sadden;
acid, antacids   France   head   bread   fled*
an Ed Ned Ted can tan sad Stan side tide/tied
dead idea acid dance *stance sadden *instead
candies *antacids distance candidates

24. **carelessness** *less ness ess ease ear mess* 67
stress fear fearless
less care earn/near clear sense *crass lease
*cease crease recess assess *caress release
careless senseless *ceaseless clearness
*crassness carelessness

25. **carnivores** *ar ane ain* (two spellings, one 68
pronunciation) *orn ove* (two pronunciations) *rain-rein
vane-vein-vain drove plain plane worn*
car scar rain rein vein vain vane move cove
rove corn acorn river raven carve *canoe crane
*ocean *senior reason *arrives *caverns carnivores

26. **carpenters** *ap ape ate et eat cheat shape* 69
skate strap
eat/ate pet net car cat cap tap tape cape
neat rate crate secret carpet scrape create repeat
escape *career *parents *partners carpenters

27. **caterpillars** *al el le ar air are* (two spellings, 70
one pronunciation) *ace* (two pronunciations)
stair-stare Word relatives: *race, racist, racial
square marble marvel parcel*
air car tar ace race pace/cape care rare spare
stare stair space trace petal rascal spiral carpet
arrest palace repair castle triple staple racist
racial pastel scalpel special capital recital plastic
elastic article particle caterpillars

28. **cauliflower** *re ful ew all ill ell ow* (two 71
pronunciations) *aw ear air are* (two spellings, one
pronunciation) *fair-fare renew refill fearful lawful*
ear air are cow low law raw few flew flaw
flow crow crew claw call fall wall well fell
fill will fair fare care fear clear awful allow
flower earful lawful caller/recall refill recoil
curfew fellow careful cauliflower

29. **celebrating** *re ing le el al eat ate* Word relatives: 72
tribe, tribal . . . repeat retreat rebate rebating
ate eat beat care cable eagle rebel bagel
angel/angle trace/crate tribe tribal create beagle
relate caring eating center central general recital
eternal beating tracing/crating creating relating
bracelet liberate triangle rectangle celebrating

30. centipedes *est ent eep *ense *seen-scene*
sent-cent-scent spent creep creepiest steepest
nice need deep seep seen dent sent cent
scent spend steep *dense *tense *scene
nicest/insect decent *descent deepest neediest
*inspected centipedes
73

31. champions *ap amp imp inch ip op stamp*
cinch skip trap
imp nap map mop hop hip chip ship shop
chop chap camp inch pinch chimp champ
chomp China panic *casino *spinach *phonics
champions
74

32. characters *ch at ash atch each beach*
mash match hatch
cat rat hat chat each/*ache cash rash trash
teach reach catch chase cheat chest *search
scratch catcher catches *trachea characters
75

33. cheerleaders **re ear eer* (two spellings, two
pronunciations) *eel eal* (two spellings, one pronunciation) *ease deer-dear heal-heel real-reel*
herd-heard sheer-shear steer stear fear grease
deer dear real reel heel heal herd heard cheer
sheer shear clear cease crease search *release
*decrease *research *rehearse cheerleaders
76

34. cholesterol *s/es oll ole* (two spellings, one
pronunciation) *ool ost* (two pronunciations)
role-roll *close-clothes frost post poll pole
cool cost lost host hero *echo hole role roll
toll troll torch close cheer cheers school secret
echoes heroes torches *clothes cholesterol
77

35. cleanliness *ness ean *ense ice *seen-scene*
price mean meanness dense
ill ice see seen nice lean clean slice alien
*sense *scene lenses Lassie *license *incense
illness niceness leanness cleanness cleanliness
78

36. communication *com tion at ount* Word relatives:
common, uncommon chat flat bat combat
at cat/act moon mount count comic comma
commit common nation motion action amount
*account *caution/*auction uncommon mountain
communication
79

25

37. community *com y ount oy ut joy shut*   80
strut amount
mom Tom nut cut coy toy Tony tiny city
mint unit unity minty mount count county
*mutiny commit community

38. comprehension *com sion ch sh ph ore ip op*   81
on (person, sermon . . .) Word relatives: *compose,*
composer . . . trip drop store common
hop hip ship chip chop shop shoe echo more
core chore shore snore score porch pooch
phone chose choir chrome choose cheers shrimp
sphere prison person poison sermon income
someone pension erosion compose composer
scorpion pioneers microphone comprehension

39. congratulations *con un uni al ist ing* (spelling   82
changes) *ot not knot plotting slingshot*
cut rot clot slot coil clog unit union uncoil
unclog artist racist casual annual caring closing
causing nursing unicorn cutting rotting tourist
contain consult contrast constant clotting
unstrung organist astronaut nocturnal continual
consultant congratulations

40. Connecticut *con uni ent one* (two pronunciations)   83
done stone phone spent
one none tone cone tent cent unit once ounce
unite union *tonic *tunic intent content *conceit
connect *continue Connecticut

41. contagious *tion in ing un ung in-inn spin*   84
swing lung spun
in inn tin sun gun stun suit song sing sung
stung sting cousin action *auction/*caution
suction contagious

42. continent *con one* (two pronunciations) *ot ote ent*   85
ice (two pronunciations) *done throne consent condone*
not cot ice one once/cone tone none note tote
tent cent nice notice content *innocent continent

43. countries *ies* (two pronunciations) *er est urse ust*   86
Word relatives: *count, recount, counter . . . purse*
trust dust dustier
corn nose nice rust crust count nurse curse
cries tries nicer nicest/insect *insert nosier
cousin *cruise counter/recount *corniest
counties countries

44. crocodiles *c ice ose* (three pronunciations) *ool*   87
Word relatives: *close, closed, closer chose those*
price school
ice rice dice lice cool rose dose lose loose
drool slice rodeo close closed closer soccer
*oriole *circle *soldier crocodiles

45. decorations *or tion o ate* Word relatives: *act, react,*   88
reaction . . . late motion potion portion
no so act date crate/react actor donor dance
dancer donate doctor indoor action tornado
cartoon senator *distance reaction *creation
*coordinates/decorations

46. democracy *y* (two pronunciations) *de *com ode*   89
oy road-rode shy joy deny destroy
cry dry Roy arm army code rode road more
adore decay decoy ready *mercy dream cream
dreamy *comedy *comrade democracy

47. destruction *un uni tion out con dis ist ent est*   90
sent-cent-scent Word relatives: *tour, tourist . . .*
conquest consent content contentment
out tie tied unit undo tour rest test tent sent
cent scent disco outer trout scout snout under
cousin detour unrest untied/united rodent outset
outside distort tourist dentist student section
suction untried contest consider contrite outcries
discount introduce reduction destruction

48. dinosaurs *un ound aid ain sun-son* Word relatives: 91
round, around . . . paid unpaid unchain unsound
us do son sun aid raid said undo rain drain
*radio *audio arson *sinus sound round around
unsaid dinosaurs

49. ducklings *ick uck ink unk ing ung brick*   92
think string truck
in ink sink link lunk luck duck dunk gunk
lick sick king sing sung lung *slung *slunk
*slink sling slick clink snuck ducklings

50. elections *tion en ice* (two pronunciations)   93
price twice men mention
ten tin ice nice lice slice elect select insect
client notice listen/enlist enclose *silence/*license
*stencil section selection/elections

51. **electricians** *eal eel een ean* (two spellings, one pronunciation) *real-reel steal-steel* Word relatives: *center, central . . . green mean heal heel*   94
eel reel real seal teen seen lean earn learn
clean steal steel screen circle *cereal center
central airline *elastic electric electricians

52. **elephants** *ph eal eel, eap eep, eat eet*   95
(two spelling patterns for all these rhymes) *heel-heal
steal-steel* Word relatives: *sleep, asleep; eat, eaten;
street squeal cheap cheep*
eat eel heel heal heat heap leap eaten phase
steal steel steep sheep sleep sleet please/asleep
planets elephants

53. **endangered** **de en ade ed eed ead* (two   96
pronunciations: *ed* and *eed*) *red-read bred bread
bleed bedspread*
Ed Ned red read/dear near dead deed need
greed dread grade danger/garden endear enrage
degree *degrade *grenade *renegade
*deranged endangered

54. **enthusiastic** *th s/es atch itch* Word relatives: 97
ten, tenth . . . scratch scratches switch switches
ten the then than thin that itch inch tenth catch
hatch snatch snitch insect itches inches stitch
stitches *suitcase *hesitant *scientist enthusiastic

55. **environment** *er ote ent* Word relatives: *mine,*   98
miner . . . quote wrote sent spent
over note vote/veto rent vent even ever never/nerve
movie event voter miner meter *meteor *motive remote
invent *reinvent *overtime environment

56. **estimating** *ing* (spelling changes) *ate it et ain*   99
ane (two spellings, one pronunciation) *main-mane*
split splitting betting imagining
sit set met time gate sane mane main gain
stain state/taste timing teasing tasting sitting
setting *imitate *imagine *instigate estimating

57. **evaporation** *tion ate ant pair-pare* Word relatives: 100
prove, proven grant chant state gate
ant ate rate rant pant pint pair pear opera
print prove proven pirate option/potion portion
*private *protein *operation evaporation

58. exhausting *ex ing* (spelling changes) *ate eight-ate site-sight* Word relatives: *six, sixth; tax, taxes . . . date dating skate skating*
ate six use/sue tax taxi gate hate site exit exist taxes/Texas sixth sight using/suing hating exhaust exhausting

101

59. fashionable *ash ish ale ail* (two spellings, one pronunciation) *an one bail-bale sale-sail lone-loan cash smash vanish Spanish*
an ban bash lash fish fail bail bale sale sail bone lone loan self shelf flash snail alone shone inhale banish *abolish fashionable

102

60. festivals *ast ist east ale ail* (two spellings, one pronunciation) *sail-sale tail-tale beast blast pail pale*
eat east fast fist list last vast vest sale sail tail tale stale/least feast *fiesta *siesta itself festivals

103

61. footballs *all ast ool oat* Word relatives: *ball, softball, footballs mall past throat pool*
ball tall toll tool fool fast last/salt solo sofa soft loft aloft float boats/boast boost/ boots blast stall stool *ballot softball footballs

104

62. fractions *ic an aint oast orn born paint panic frantic*
an ran fist cost corn faint saint craft first facts sonic tonic arson coast roast acorn scorn *casino *factor fractions

105

63. frightening *ing ight eight ine ire ief* Word relatives: *nine, ninth . . . weight chief shine shining*
tire hire fire fine nine ninth tiger thief grief eight right fight fright firing hiring *ignite *inherit freight frighten frightening

106

64. geography *a (ago, yoga) ph age ape ope scrape stage slope scope*
go ago age rage page/gape yoga ahoy hero gore rope hope grope grape *gorge *opera graph *gopher geography

107

65. governments *ment s/es een ong ove* (two 108
pronunciations) Word relatives: *move, remove,
movers . . . prove drove wrong movement*
go see seen teen song goes veto move
stove grove green greet remove movers vetoes
strong monster segment governs governments

66. grandchildren *ed ing en er and ead* (two 109
pronunciations) *herd-heard* Word relatives: *grandchild,
grandchildren . . . bead thread hiding grandstand*
and hid hide care land hang dine head read
lead hard herd hear heard dread diner dined
cared child dance anger/range ranger danger hanger
dinner danced landed ending caring harden hidden
hearing landing dancing darling grannie earring
children grandchild grandchildren

67. grandfathers *aft age ange great-grate* 110
Word relatives: *stage, stagehand; father, grandfathers;
page cage wages crafts*
gas age rage raft draft after range great/grate
stage father strange arrange rafters gardens
*transfer *stagehand grandfathers

68. grandmothers *ame oan one* (two pronunciations, 111
two spellings) *none shame lone loan*
one done tone game name same tame moan
groan other horse stone drone throne dragon
garden mother another armrest grandmothers

69. greenhouse *g ung ug ough our-hour tough* 112
lug lung strung
go rug hug our hour goes gone hung rung
sung/snug shoe huge house horse shrug green
rough enough hunger *surgeon *generous greenhouse

70. gymnastics *g y ic ain rain rainy brainy maintain* 113
gas gym gain sign mint mist misty minty stain
magic manic giant nasty *antics sanity stingy
*assign gymnast gymnastics

71. handicapped *ed* (spelling changes) *c/ch ain ane* 114
inch ip pain-pane cinch ship shipped slipped
nap dip chip dine hide pain pane cane *ache
acid idea inch pinch chain/China dined *panic
panda dance napped dipped chipped pinched
handicapped

72. **hibernation** *in it one* (two pronunciations) *ore oar*   115
(two spellings, one pronunciation) *air-heir bear-bare*
bore-boar birth-berth or-ore-oar Word relatives: *nine,*
ninth; in, inner; done stone roar shore
or ore oar one bit hit air heir herb born
horn bear/bare bore boar none bone tone tore
nine ninth inner habit orbit birth berth Bertha
orient throne hornet obtain retain/retina intern
inborn inhabit inherit inertia baritone hibernation

73. **hippopotamus** *s/sh oop oot out outh ump boots*   116
troop trout trump
out pout push pump thump stump stamp stomp
stoop hoops hoots/shoot shout spout mouth south
*photo *smooth *shampoo hippopotamus

74. **immigrants** *ing* (spelling changes) *g am an im in*   117
swim swimming plan planning
an tan tin Tim rim ram gram grim trim grin
grain grant grits giant margin rating mating/taming
timing ramming trimming migrants immigrants

75. **independence** *ed* (spelling changes) *de eed end*   118
Word relatives: *depend, dependence, independence;*
greed spend defend defended
end pen pin die ice iced died need deed deep
dine dined ended pinned penned needed depend
denied deepen deepened dependence independence

76. **ingredients** *ed ing er ing* Word relatives: *design,*   119
redesign; sing, singer . . . ring fling string ringer
sing/sign grin dine diner enter sting dinner dining
desire singer/signer *resign *design insert stinger
grinned desiring entering inserted inserting *redesign
*ringside ingredients

77. **inspectors** *c er-est ice* (two pronunciations) *ent*   120
cent-sent-scent Word relatives: *inspect, inspectors;*
nose, nosier . . . rice twice invent indent
one once nose nice rent sent cent scent
price coins nicer nicest notice nosier insert
insect inspect nosiest stepson *protein *process
*princess inspectors

78. **interception** *inter re en pro* *tion *o ent*   121
Word relatives: *intercept, interception; repent*
motion promotion protection
no pro tent cent enter entire entice encore
center/recent recipe protest protect percent
Internet *reception *retention *repetition *recipient
intercept interception

79. **interference** *inter re en ee ence ire in-inn*   122
Word relatives: *interfere, interference; retire, retiree;*
three rewire require sentence
in inn fee tee tree free fire tire fence enter
entire entice recent *recite retire retiree referee
*inference interfere interference

80. **interviews** *in re wr est ire infest request*   123
require inspire
new view west nest rest tire wire write wrist
renew entire invite invent invest *invert *insert
viewer/review revise *reinvest interviews

81. **invitations** *tion sion o an in-inn motion lotion*   124
notion mansion
go so an in inn tan ants/Stan stain/saint/satin
toast visit vision station instant invasion
invitations

82. **kilometer**s *ime ilk ike oke prime joke*   125
choke spike
like Mike milk silk slim time lime slime smoke
stoke meter meteor/remote *stereo strike stroke
liters *loiters *omelets kilometers

83. **kindhearted** *kn en ed ank ink ead* (two   126
pronunciations) *there-their* Word relatives: *hard, harden,*
hardened; plead bead bread spread
hid hard dark rank rink head dead read knit
knee knead *dread drink drank thank think there
their thread darken harden hidden *either *neither
redhead darkened hardened kindhearted

84. **libraries** *ail ale* (two spellings, one pronunciation) *are*   127
(two pronunciations) *sail-sale bail-bale trail jail*
snail scale
ear/are air ail ale sale sail rail bail bale base
bare rare labs/slab *laser *barrel *rabies libraries

85. literature *le eat ee ie tea-tee die heat*   128
beetle steeple
eat lie tie tea tee tree late later treat
trial/trail title liter litter letter turtle rattle
trailer retreat literature

86. lumberjacks *able le ark ack uck break-brake*   129
Word relatives: *bake, baker; lumber, lumberjacks;*
struck buckle chuckle packable
use cure sack lack rack back buck luck
*muck bark lark bake brake/break baker
*muscle marble/ramble rumble/lumber usable
curable crumble lumberjacks

87. magazines *g ag age* (two pronunciations) *aze*   130
Word relatives: *amaze, amazing; blaze cage*
bag baggage
man men gem nag zag zig age sage zing
sing/sign size gaze maze amaze image manage
amazing *amnesia magazines

88. mathematics *s/es ic ash itch eam est* Word   131
relatives: *match, matches . . . west cream switch*
switches
mat mats math mash cash itch team test
chest steam/teams match attic static stitch
itches attach matches attaches mathematics

89. measuring *sure ing g ue ug plug shrug*   132
glue gluing
rug mug/gum gem use/sue sure germ amuse
argue using/suing margin manger *mirage *genius
insure amusing erasing *geraniums measuring

90. meteorologists *less er/est s/es ist er oom oot*   133
Word relatives: *motor, motorists . . . doom bloom*
shoot shooter
go sit time tire goes solo loot root room
gloom igloo timer moist motto motor storm
settle sitter goriest gooier gooiest mottoes
looters soloist legroom moister moistest gloomier
roomiest timeless tireless rootless termites
settlers tortoise tortoises motorists stormiest
gloomiest mistletoe meteorologists

91. millimeters *er ell ill ile ime* Word relatives: 134
slime, slimier; sell, resell, seller . . . chill chillier
grime grimier
sell tell till mill time tile mile/lime
slime/miles/smile still smell resell/seller *trellis
*sterile sillier slimier smellier millimeters

92. Milwaukee *eak eek* (two spellings, one pronunciation) 135
ake ike we-wee weak-week mail-male leak-leek
peak peek creek creak
we wee weak/wake make lake/leak leek week
*meek meal/male mail mile Mike like alike
*leukemia Milwaukee

93. Minnesota *in ine one* (two pronunciations) *ame* 136
ane ain (two spellings, one pronunciation) *main-mane*
phone done spine incline
in tin ten ate one none tone/note sane
mane/name same tame/mate main stain stone
insane inmate tennis *nominate Minnesota

94. misunderstood *mis ous ness s/es ess oss* 137
miner-minor Word relatives: *tour, tourism;*
mine, miner . . . less bless cross crossness
use sun mud mood mess moss toss tour
room riot mine miner minor minus dress dries
misuse sunset sunrise monster stories studies
minuses tourism serious riotous monstrous
enormous roominess moodiness muddiness
understood misunderstood

95. mockingbirds *ink ick ock* Word relatives: 138
king, kingdom; stick stink shrink shock
ink sink mink rink risk king sick sock
rock dock bird smock brick brisk brink
drink bingo kingdom songbird mockingbirds

96. mosquitoes *mis qu it ue sum-some* 139
Word relatives: *use, misuse; quote, misquote; split*
cue misfit miscue
sit use/sue sum some toes omit emit quit
quite/quiet quest quote mouse moose issue
tissue misuse misquote mosquitoes

97. multiplying *y (two pronunciations) ly*   140
(spelling changes) um ump Word relatives:
glum, glumly . . . strum grump grumpy grumpily
my ply ump gum glum plum pity puny ugly
tiny lily mint lump lumpy minty guilt typing
glumly lumpily guiltily multiply multiplying

98. mysteries *y (two pronunciations) y-i I-eye cry*   141
cries dry driest
I eye try sty stem mess miss mist misty
messy tries sties miser misery sister/resist
*series *system messier mysteries

99. neighborhood *ed ide idge ind ore hi-high*   142
hire-higher Word relatives: *high, higher . . . glide*
glided mind beside
hi high hire bore gore bind ride ridge bored
*honor rodeo grind bride bridge higher behind
*region/ignore ignored *honored neighborhood

100. newspapers *ap aw ear* (two pronunciations)   143
wr rap-wrap wars-warp-warn Word relatives: *news,*
renew; paper, newspapers; warm wart year bear
are/ear saw paw raw rap wrap/warp warn
wars were wren near pear wear snap news
renew *swear spear paper seesaw *answer
snapper newspapers

101. nutrition *tion ot ut out scout shot shut shout*   144
out not nut rut rot riot unit into noun
ruin tour trot trout union tuition nutrition

102. outfielders *out de re er/est use old ild ile*   145
ide oil tied/tide Word relatives: *field, outfield,*
outfielders . . . scold coil recoil amuse
us use old oil tie tied/tide told fold foul foil
toil soil loud ride side tile file filed/field slide
older outer reset reuse refuse retold refold
relief result oldest louder forest/foster defuse
desire detour desert defrost loudest outside
outfield outfielders

103. perpendicular *pre ed* (spelling changes) *al el le*   146
il ap ace peace-piece plane-plain Word relatives:
rip, ripped . . . trap trapped trace traced
rip lap clap race pace duel cruel pedal rural
repel panel plane plain place raced pupil peril
peace piece uncle purple ripple nipple candle
cradle curdle cereal denial pencil parcel placed
ripped lapped clapped replace cripple prepare
prepaid preplan pelican audience perpendicular

104. Philadelphia *ead* (two pronunciations) *all ill ale*   147
ail (two spellings, one pronunciation) *hail-hale pail-pale*
led-lead spread thread bale-bail
Ed led all ill pill hill hall hail pail pale hale
idea head lead plead/pedal ahead apple *appeal
*applied Philadelphia

105. photosynthesis *ph y y-ies, iest ist one*   148
Word relatives: *shy, shiest, shyness . . . spry throne
cyclone cyclist*
spy shy pony spot nose nosy type host noise
noisy shine shiny stone stony photo phone phony
spies snoop snoopy ponies shiest spotty typist
tiptoe python honest honesty typhoon stepson
phoniest hostess shyness hypnosis hypnotist
hypothesis photosynthesis

106. Pittsburgh *ight ush* (two pronunciations) *ust urt*   149
Word relatives: *tight, uptight . . . crush flight
crust blurt*
sir stir rust gust bust bush push rush gush
hurt spurt shirt brush sight right tight trust
bright *upright *uptight Pittsburgh

107. pneumonia *an ap ane ain en in ine pain-pane*   150
main-mane happen napkin insane maintain
in an pan/nap nip/pin pen men man map/Pam
nine mine pine pane pain main mane/mean
moan open upon pneumonia

108. poinsettias *ain ane* (two spellings, one pronunciation)   151
an pain-pane Word relatives: *piano, pianist; crane
sprain plain plane*
tan pan span sane pane pain Spain stain point
piano ponies pities season siesta tiptoe teapot
stepson pianist petition poinsettias

109. **pollutants** *ant ast oll out sun-son stroll blast* 152
  sprout chant
  sun son out ant aunt pant past last pout poll
  toll also upon slant plant spout stout snout
  pants *total *postal pollutants

110. **precipitation** *re tion ic ot* Word relatives: *poet,* 153
  poetic . . . pro plot picnic fiction friction
  not pot poet topic tonic panic attic tropic
  poetic action caption protect protein propane
  patriot apricot petition creation traction reaction
  reappoint patriotic precipitation

111. **presidents** *dis pre re ness ess end ent ide* 154
  pride-pried peer-pier Word relatives: *preside,*
  presidents; side, sidestep . . . distress wide
  wideness beside
  end send sent dent side peer pier spend spent
  dress press pride/pried tried/tired resist resent
  reside entire desert dessert preside pretend
  present/serpent depress redness ripeness dispense
  disperse resident sidestep tiredness presidents

112. **psychologist** *co ist ly ool oop ost* (two 155
  pronunciations) Word relatives: *cost, costly . . .*
  scoop frost most mostly
  pool loop hoop solo cost lost post host ghost
  pilot stoop stool school cohost gossip costly
  ghostly copilot soloist psychologist

113. **rattlesnakes** *ness ank ate ake eak eat eal* 156
  eel eet real-reel steel-steal Word relatives: *snake,*
  rattlesnakes; eat, anteater . . . prank flake
  weak weakness
  ate/eat neat seat late rate rank sank tank
  lake/leak teak teal seal real reel steel steal
  stank ankle treat sneak/snake skate sleet skeet
  alert/alter street anteater translate lateness
  realness alertness alternate rattlesnakes

114. **rectangles** *re en al/el/le er/est ate steel-steal* 157
  Word relatives: *angle, rectangles; center, central . . .*
  date gate state rebate
  lean late later large steal steel clean eagle
  easel angel/angle react enact crate create relate
  resale recent/center castle gentle cereal enrage
  senate leaner leanest largest enlarge reenact
  neglect central eternal general elegant cleaner
  cleanest sergeant strangle rectangles

115. refreshments *re ent est ee* Word relatives: *fresh, freshmen, refresh . . . spree spent repent request* 158
see fee free tree nest rest rent sent them then these three enter fresh reset refer resent reenter refresh freshmen *semester *freshener refreshments

116. relatives *re al el eal deal squeal repeal rebel* 159
set seal real steal trial rival vital easel reset relive reseal reveal revise travel *several *versatile/relatives

117. relaxation *ex ax tion one oan* (two spellings, one pronunciation) *loan-lone alter-altar* Word relatives: *relax, relaxation; ox, oxen; lone, alone; wax zone phone moan* 160
ax ox tax lax oxen exit taxi tone lone loan roan alone alert/alter altar relax extra *liter *loiter *elation relation relaxation

118. reporters *ee est ose ort re* Word relatives: *port, report, reporters . . . those quest request retest* 161
see tree rest pest rose pose post port sort sport spree error terror stereo poster pester report resort restore reporters

119. responsible *ible re ess oss* Word relatives: *lion, lioness; sense, sensible . . . cross across stress recess* 162
lion bone ripe boss loss less bless sense rebel reopen relies replies lioness boneless ripeness sensible possible response responsible

120. rhinoceros *c/ch* (four sounds) *s/es ore* Word relatives: *hero, heroic; shore, onshore . . . score adore before enriches* 163
one once nice inch rich hero echo core chore shore snore choir chose choose inches riches heroic enrich corner *cornier onshore *erosion *schooner rhinoceros

121. scientists *est* (spelling changes) *ent ice sent-cent-scent* Word relatives: *ice, iciest, iciness . . . spent spice spiciest spiciness* 164
ice nice tent test nest/sent cent scent since insect insist nicest cities/iciest iciness tiniest scientists

122. scoreboard *ed* (spelling changes) *oar ore soar-sore bore-boar board-bored border-boarder* Word relatives: *board, boarder . . . star starred adored scored*   165

bar soar sore core bore boar roar scar scare
board bored score adore rodeo scared/*sacred
record barred *border *boarder scarred scoreboard

123. semifinals *ame ale ail ile* (two pronunciations) *sale-sail male-mail* Word relatives: *flame, inflame; frame became while reptile*   166

name fame same sale male mail sail nail fail
file mile smile/slime snail flame final aliens
Lassie *inflame *missile *families semifinals

124. sensational *tion en al el s/es* Word relatives: *season, seasonal . . . mention motion option optional*   167

lies ties atlas *alias nasal steal stole stolen
listen/tinsel tassel enlist entail nation season
atlases *aliases seasonal national toenails
sensation sensational

125. skateboarding *ain age ank ask ate ait oar ore oak oke* (two pronunciations for *ain, age* and two spelling patterns for rhymes *ate, ait; oar, ore; oak, oke) *bore-boar soar-sore gait-gate* Word relatives: *store, storage . . . page package maintain captain*   168

ate age ask oak soak rage rate date gate
gait bait rain rank sank task bore boar soar
sore store skate stage stain brain drain again
orbit broke stoke stroke donate bandit basket
ignore bargain against sandbag senator storage
bandage sabotage drainage skateboarding

126. snowstorm *ow* (two pronunciations) *oon to-too-two* Word relatives: *snow, storm, snowstorm; chow flow throw below*   169

to two too moo mow row tow sow now snow
stow soon moon worm worst motor swoon
storm snowstorm

127. spectacular *ture ause ap ue us ute use* *acc-accept, accuse, accurate strap rapture because applause*   170

us use/sue cue true cute plus trap slap super
atlas pause cause clause cactus accept accuse
salute capture pasture *accurate spectacular

128. subtracting *ing* (spelling changes) *ang ing ung*
ub Word relatives: *sing, sang, sung . . . hang hung*
club clubbing
bat cut rub sub stub rang rung ring sing sang
sung stung stunt sting scrub scuba guitar string
strung *strict strain *static *tragic batting cutting
*curtains subtracting

171

129. teammates *ame ate eat eam see-sea tea-tee*
meat-meet Word relatives: *team, mate, teammates;*
cheat treat retreat repeat
at ate/eat tea tee see sea seat/east team/tame
mate/meat meet same taste/state steam estate
teammates

172

130. telescopes *eep ope oss ost* (two pronunciations)
Word relatives: *sleep, slept keep kept creep crept*
toes toss loss lots lost cost post/spot/stop cope
slope elope sleet sleep steep slept closet select
steeple telescopes

173

131. thousands *and out ot ut ound sh scout found*
rebound grandstand
and out not hot hut nut hunt hand sand shut
shot aunt *haunt snout shout/south sound hound
stand donuts *handouts thousands

174

132. toothbrushes *s/es ush* (two pronunciations) *ust*
our-hour Word relatives: *rush, rushes . . . push*
pushes rush rushes
our hour *hobo rust rush hush bush brush
tours usher trust thrust robust outset *hoboes
horses rushes bushes brushes *booster *hothouse
toothbrushes

175

133. tournaments *er or ment ture out et meet-meat*
sore-soar Word relatives: *tune, tuner . . . outset outlet*
ferment mixture
set met meet meat sore soar tune tuner tumor
tutor toast outran outset nature mature *stature
toaster monster senator *torment ornament
outsmart tournaments

176

134. traditions *and oad oast* Word relatives: *riot,*
antiriot coast load grand grandstand
ant and sand road toad riot/trio radio *ratio
toast roast stand strand raisin distant station
*antiriot traditions

177

135. triangles *al/le/el* (three spellings, one pronunciation)   178
ale ail tail-tale bail bale mail male
nail rail tail tale stale trial/trail giant alien snail
angel/angle tangle tingle tinsel rental signal single
*gristle *strangle triangles

136. unconscious *con uni on* (two pronunciations) *oon*   179
son-sun contest uniform bonbons monsoon
on con son sun noun noon soon cuss coin
coins sinus sonic onion onions unions/*unison
cousins conscious *concussion unconscious

137. underdogs *under ound ude udge urge do-due*   180
Word relatives: *do, undo, redo . . . fudge purge
hound underground*
do due end send undo redo rude dude urge
surge under sound round nudge *drudge ground
sudden *surgeon undergo rounded underdogs

138. undernourished *under re ed er en un*   181
Word relatives: *shred, shredder* (spelling changes) . . .
stun stunned gun gunner
red run sun use done hide ride rise user/sure
shun under rider riser rerun order union shred
hidden redden insure ensure endure runner desire
desired shunned hundred hideous reunion disorder
shredder underside underdone nourished surrounded
undernourished

139. unemployment *ment y* (two pronunciations) *oy et*   182
elt Word relatives: *employ, employment, unemployment;
enjoy enjoyment payment shipment*
my ply toy yet pet met melt pelt pony only
type nylon penny money empty enemy lumpy
plenty employ moment *monument employment
unemployment

140. unfortunate *un ture en* (spelling changes) *ot une*   183
for-four Word relatives: *fat, fatten, nonfat . . . got
gotten mixture capture*
fat rot not out for four true tune dune often
rotten fatten nonfat future nature untrue outrun
turnout fortune fortunate unfortunate

141. unpredictable *un pre de en ence able ible ude* 184
Word relatives: *prudent, prudence . . . enter delude*
prepaid unendurable
act cut cure rude crude prude decal enact
uncle unpaid unreal unable entire entice endure
endear precut edible derail detail detain debate
depart decent decline unclear include intrude
curable pretend predict prudent prudence patience
audience credible unrelated endurable unpredictable

142. unsatisfactory *y* (two pronunciations) *out un uni* 185
tion ist ic our (three pronunciations) Word relatives:
satisfy, satisfactory . . . unicorn fiction friction typist
nut art our sour four your tour rain fuss unit
unity unify rainy nutty fussy attic scour unfit
unfair static outfit outran outcry artist tourist
outcast factory satisfy caution/auction station frantic
raincoat fraction traction fantastic astronaut
stationary satisfactory unsatisfactory

143. unsuccessful *ful elf un use ue* Word relatives: 186
use, useful . . . true untrue useless clueless
fun sun use/sue cue elf self less fuss fuse
clue fuel uncle unless useful success successful
unsuccessful

144. vaccination *tion con ic an on in-inn can-cannot* 187
sonic manic friction conviction
on in inn Ann ant/tan van can con act into
tonic antic civic cannot *vacant action nation
contain *convict vacation *aviation vaccination

145. vegetarians *in ing* (spelling changes) *age* (two 188
pronunciations) *ive* (two pronunciations) *see-sea;*
great-grate; vein-vain-vane; rain-rein-reign
Word relatives: *serve, servant . . . drive driving*
raging image
see sea give save rave rage vine/vein vain
vane rain rein reign great/grate tease serve
train again invent invest invert insert strive
native enrage starve raving saving savage
ravage average against teasing serving veteran
vinegar vagrant servant sergeant trainees
starving negative navigate vegetarians

146. veterinarian *in re ain ent* Word relatives: 189
*train, trainer, trainee, retrain . . . indent resent
remain regain*
rent vent rain ever never/nerve train event
invent invite entire retire retain retrain/trainer
*trainee *terrain veteran *retainer veterinarian

147. vocabulary *ab ob ub by-buy* Word relatives: 190
curl, curly; shrub snob grab grub
by buy boa rob rub cub cob cab crab club
ruby/bury curb curl curly cobra royal labor
Carol/coral cavalry vocabulary

148. volcanoes *ave one oon ove* (two pronunciations)   191
Word relatives: *volcano, volcanoes; one, once . . .
brave stove stone spoon*
one once/cone lone soon loon love cove save
slave/salve solve/loves alone ocean canoe *salon
*saloon cloves *alcove volcano volcanoes

149. volleyballs *able ell ob* Word relatives: *love,*   192
*lovely, lovable; volley, volleyballs . . . smell snob
throb hobnob*
sob lob slob ball bell sell yell ally love above
solve belly alley valley *volley/lovely lovable
solvable *syllable volleyballs

150. wilderness *less ness ed end* Word relatives: 193
*wild, wildness, wilderness . . . shred trend
trendiness slenderness*
end red wed/dew win wind wild wire lend
*idle weird slender winless endless redness
wildness *idleness *dewiness wireless windless
weirdness wilderness

LESSON 1

LETTERS

aeiccdnst

MAKE

end	tied/	dance	insect	instead	distance	accidents
and	tide/		*stance	candies		
ant	diet/		*antics			
die	edit		*scenic			
tie	send					
	tend					

SORT

ance   end   ie   tide/tied

TRANSFER

lie   bend   spend   France

LETTERS

a e o u u d n r s t v

MAKE

end	send	trend	detour	*arduous	*ravenous	adventurous
	tend	sound	nature	treason		
	tour	round	around	astound		
			starve	nervous		
			reason			

SORT

ous   end   ound

TRANSFER

lend   spend   found   ground

LESSON 3

LETTERS

aaiogllrst

MAKE

go	ago	gill	*ratio	stroll	gorillas	alligators
	all	tall	atlas	sailor		
	ill	toll	*alias			
		also	troll			
		riot/	grill			
		*trio	still			
			girls			
			solar			

SORT

all   ill   oll

TRANSFER

poll   kill   drill   squall

LESSON 4

LETTERS

a e e d m m n n s t

MAKE

man	Stan	named	teased/	amendments
men	seat	*dense	seated	
ten	neat	*tense	*senate	
tan	meat	tease	tanned	
	meet		manned	
	name			

SORT

ed (spelling changes)   an   en   eat
meat-meet

TRANSFER

when   beat   plan   planned

47

LESSON 5

LETTERS

a a e i c m n r s

MAKE

arm	mace	cream	maniac	marines/	*amnesiac	Americans
ace	race	mania	*anemia	remains		
			*anemic	*arsenic		
			camera	America		
			scream	*amnesia		
			armies			
			racism			
			marina			

SORT

ace   eam

Word relatives: anemia, anemic . . .

TRANSFER

space   place   dream   stream

LETTERS

a a i i b h m n p s

MAKE

arm	ship	smash	*banish	amphibians
Sam	snip		*mishap	
ham	snap			
has/	bash			
ash	mash			
map				
nap				
sap				
sip				

SORT

am   ap   ash   ip

TRANSFER

crash   whip   slap   cram

LESSON 7

LETTERS

a a e i y n n r r s v

MAKE

rain*	yearn	*ravine	anniversary
rein	river	*arisen	
vein	arena	arrive	
vain	arise	insane	
vane		navies	
sane		varies	
very			
vary			
navy			
area			
earn			

SORT

y-ies   ain   ane (two spellings, one pronunciation)

rain-rein   vain-vane-vein

a-area, arena, arise, arisen, arrive

TRANSFER

gain   crane   plain   plane (check in dictionary)

LETTERS

a i i i o b c n s t t

MAKE

act	ants	coats/	static	station	antibiotics
ant	boat	coast	action	*Titanic	
	coat	boast			
		toast		*botanist	
		bacon			
		basic			
		tonic			
		sonic			
		attic			

SORT

tion   ic   oat   oast

TRANSFER

roast   picnic   fiction   friction

LESSON 9

a a o u n r s s t t

MAKE

art	sour	stunt	astronauts
out	sort	start	
nut	tart	*snort	
rut	rust	trust/	
run	stun	strut	
sun		trout	
son		*stout	
our		*snout	

SORT

art   *ort   our   out   ut   ust   un   sun-son

TRANSFER

shout   short   scour   outsmart

52

LETTERS

a a a i u l r s t

MAKE

sir	star	trail/	Austria	Australia
sit	stir	trial		
sat	slit/	*atlas		
rat/	list	*ultra		
tar	Asia			
	sail			
	tail			
	rail			

SORT

at   ar   ail   it   ir

Asia, Austria, Australia

TRANSFER

fail   brat   jar   quit

LESSON 11

LETTERS

a i o b d m n n t

MAKE

it	bit	mind	*baton	bandit	*dominant	badminton
	bat	bind	nomad	nation		
	mat	into	admit			
	mad	*atom				
	bad	lamb				
		tomb				
		omit				

SORT

ad   at   it   ind

words ending in *mb*

TRANSFER

grind   glad   split   flat

LETTERS

a e i o b l m r t

MAKE

oil	tore	broil	tribal	Baltimore
ore	bore	trail/	*timber	
	more/	trial	*limber	
	Rome	tribe	*mobile	
	mile			
	tile			
	lamb			
	limb			
	tomb			
	toil			
	boil			

SORT

ore oil ile
words ending in *mb*

TRANSFER

smile spoil chore shore

LESSON 13

LETTERS

a e e o b m r s t t

MAKE

be	bee	Bart	beast	stream	*armrest	barometers
	art	roam	boast	remote		
		Rome	roast	rebate		
		tomb	smart	resort		
		east	steam	*arrest		

SORT

re   art   east   oast
be-bee   roam-Rome

TRANSFER

least   toast   chart   restart

LETTERS

a e i u u b f l t

MAKE

at	fat	belt	table	beautiful
	eat/	felt	fable	
	ate	fail	*built	
	bat	blue/		
	bet	lube		
		tube		
		fate		
		late/		
		tale		
		tail		
		bail		
		bale/		
		able		

SORT

at   ate   ale ail (one pronunciation, two spellings)   elt
bale-bail   tail-tale

TRANSFER

melt   state   mail male (check in dictionary)

L E T T E R S

a i o y b g h p r

M A K E

by	pry	bray	hairy	*phobia	biography
	pro	pray	graph		
	boa	gray			
	Roy	grab			
	boy	*orgy			
	bay	ahoy			
		hair			

S O R T

ph   y (two pronunciations)   ay   oy

T R A N S F E R

sky   stray   joy   shy

LETTERS

a i y b d h r s t

MAKE

day	tray	hairy	*radish	birthdays
shy	bird	dairy/		
try	dirt	diary		
	yard	daisy		
	tidy	dirty		
	hair	*tardy		
		third		
		shirt		
		stray		

SORT

y (two pronunciations)   ay   irt   ird

TRANSFER

squirt   flirt   flirty   spray

LESSON 17

LETTERS

a i b b c d k l r s

MAKE

ask	skid	slick	blackbirds
kid	slid	slack	
	bald	black	
	said	brick	
	risk	brisk	
	bark		
	dark		
	lark		
	lack		
	rack		
	back		
	lick		
	sick		

SORT

ark   ack   ick   id

TRANSFER

stack   stick   spark   slid

LETTERS

a i b d l r s z z

MAKE

bad	labs/	braid/	*lizard	blizzards
sad	slab	*rabid		
lad	drab	*dials		
lid	Brad			
bid	bird			
rid	bald			
lab	raid			

SORT

ad   id   ab   aid

TRANSFER

paid   afraid   skid   crab

LETTERS

e o o o b k r s t

MAKE

or	ore	sore	roost	stroke	booster	bookstore
		tore	boost	robots		
		took	brook	retook		
		book	store			
		boot	broke			
		root	stoke			

SORT

ook   oot   oost   oke   ore

or-ore

TRANSFER

shoot   shore   joke   cookbook

LESSON 20

LETTERS

a e o u b g h h k r r s t

This can be a two-day lesson, or pick and choose some *words.*

MAKE

use/	rage	argue	hoarse	through	outbreak	breakthroughs
sue	bake	rough	streak	brought	shortage	
hue	beak	tough	bought	hostage		
age	teak	ought	sought	storage	surrogate	
	true	stage	though	outrage		
		usage				
		store				
		short				
		brake/				
		break				
		steak/				
		stake				
		horse				

SORT

ake   eak (two pronunciations)   age (two pronunciations)

ough   ought   ue

brake-break   steak-stake   horse-hoarse

Word relatives: store, storage; use, usage . . .

TRANSFER

thought   glue   leak   lake

63

LESSON 21

LETTERS

eiubfghllrt

MAKE

big	bull	fight	bright	fighter	bullfighter
beg	full	light	fright		
bug	fill	right	flight		
	fell		*thrill		
	bell		refill		
	bill		*bullet		

SORT

er   ell   ill   ull   ight
Word relatives: fill, refill . . .

TRANSFER

pull   spill   shell   lighter

LETTERS

aaoucllrst

MAKE

call	clout	stroll	coastal	calculators
tall	coral	rascal	*callous	
toll	stall	*actual		
roll	atlas	*casual		
also	court	cactus		
clot	troll	crocus		

SORT

al   all   oll

TRANSFER

mall   poll   scroll   small

LESSON 23

LETTERS

a a e i c d d n s t

MAKE

an	Ned	Stan	dance	*stance	*instead	*antacids	candidates
Ed	Ted	side		sadden	candies	distance	
	can	tide/					
	tan	tied					
	sad	dead					
		idea					
		acid					

SORT

c   an   ance   ed *ead (two spellings, one pronunciation)   ide
tide-tied
Word relatives: sad, sadden; acid, antacids

TRANSFER

France   head   bread fled (check in dictionary)

LETTERS

a e e e c l n r s s s

MAKE

less	clear	crease	release	senseless	carelessness
care	sense	recess		*ceaseless	
earn/	*crass	assess	careless	clearness	
near	lease	*caress		*crassness	
	*cease				

SORT

less ness ess ease ear

TRANSFER

mess stress fear fearless

LESSON 25

LETTERS

a e i o c n r r s v

MAKE

car	scar	acorn	*senior	*arrives	carnivores
	rain	river	reason	*caverns	
	rein	raven			
	vein	carve			
	vain	*canoe			
	vane	crane			
	move	*ocean			
	cove				
	rove				
	corn				

SORT

ar   ane ain (two spellings, one pronunciation)

orn   ove (two pronunciations)

rain-rein   vane-vein-vain

TRANSFER

drove   plain plane (check in dictionary)   worn

LETTERS

a e e c n p r r s t

MAKE

eat/	tape	crate	secret	*parents	*partners	carpenters
ate	cape		carpet			
pet	neat		scrape			
net	rate		create			
car			repeat			
cat			escape			
cap			*career			
tap						

SORT

ap   ape   ate   et   eat

TRANSFER

cheat   shape   skate   strap

LESSON 27

LETTERS

a a e i c l l p r r s t

This can be a two-day lesson, or pick and choose some words.

MAKE

air	race	spare	rascal	scalpel	particle	caterpillars
car	pace/	stare	spiral	special		
tar	cape	stair	carpet	capital		
ace	care	space	arrest	recital		
	rare	trace	palace	plastic		
		petal	repair	elastic		
			castle	article		
			triple			
			staple			
			racist			
			racial			
			pastel			

SORT

al   el   le   ar   air are (two spellings, one pronunciation)
ace (two pronunciations)
stair-stare
Word relatives: race, racist, racial

TRANSFER

square   marble   marvel   parcel (check all in dictionary)

LETTERS

a e i o u c f l l r w

This can be a two-day lesson, or pick and choose some words.

MAKE

ear	flew	well	clear	flower	careful	cauliflower
air	flaw	fell	awful	earful		
are	flow	fill	allow	lawful		
cow	crow	will		caller/		
low	crew	fair		recall		
law	claw	fare		refill		
raw	call	care		recoil		
few	fall	fear		curfew		
	wall			fellow		

SORT

re   ful   ew   all   ill   ell   ow (two pronunciations)   aw

ear   air   are (two spellings, one pronunciation)

fair-fare

Point out that *re* sometimes means "back" or "again."

TRANSFER

renew   refill   fearful   lawful

LESSON 29

a e e i b c g l n r t

This can be a two-day lesson, or pick and choose some words.

MAKE

ate	beat	cable	tribal	central	creating	rectangle	celebrating
eat	care	eagle	create	general	relating		
		rebel	beagle	recital	bracelet		
		bagel	relate	eternal	liberate		
		angel/	caring	beating	triangle		
		angle	eating	tracing/			
		trace/	center	crating			
		crate					
		tribe					

SORT

re   ing   le   el   al   eat   ate
Word relatives: tribe, tribal . . .

TRANSFER

repeat   retreat   rebate   rebating

72

LETTERS

e e e i c d n p s t

MAKE

nice	scent	nicest/	*descent	neediest	centipedes
need	spend	insect	deepest		
deep	steep	decent		*inspected	
seep	*dense				
seen	*tense				
dent	*scene				
sent					
cent					

SORT

est   ent   eep   *ense
*seen-scene   sent-cent-scent

TRANSFER

spent   creep   creepiest   steepest

LETTERS

a i o c h m n p s

MAKE

imp	chip	pinch	*casino	*spinach	champions
nap	ship	chimp		*phonics	
map	shop	champ			
mop	chop	chomp			
hop	chap	China			
hip	camp	panic			
	inch				

SORT

ap   amp   imp   inch   ip   op

TRANSFER

stamp   cinch   skip   trap

74

LETTERS

a a e c c h r r s t

MAKE

cat	chat	trash	*search	scratch	characters
rat	each/	teach		catcher	
hat	*ache	reach		catches	
	cash	catch		*trachea	
	rash	chase			
		cheat			
		chest			

SORT

ch   at   ash   atch   each

TRANSFER

beach   mash   match   hatch

75

LESSON 33

LETTERS

a e e e e c d h l r r s

MAKE

deer	heard	crease	*release	*decrease	cheerleaders
dear	cheer	search		*research	
real	sheer			*rehearse	
reel	shear				
heel	clear				
heal	cease				
herd					

SORT

*re   ear eer (two spellings, one pronunciation)

eel eal (two spellings, one pronunciation)   ease

deer-dear   heal-heel   real-reel   herd-heard   sheer-shear

TRANSFER

steer stear fear (check in dictionary)   grease

76

LETTERS

e e o o c h l l r s t

MAKE

cool	troll	cheers	torches	cholesterol
cost	torch	school	*clothes	
lost	close	secret		
host	cheer	select		
hero		echoes		
*echo		heroes		
hole				
role				
roll				
toll				

SORT

s/es   oll ole (two spellings, one pronunciation)

ool   ost (two pronunciations)

role-roll   *close-clothes

TRANSFER

frost   post   poll pole (check in dictionary)

LESSON 35

LETTERS

a e e i c l l n n s s

MAKE

ill	seen	clean	lenses	*license	niceness	cleanliness
ice	nice	slice	Lassie	*incense	leanness	
see	lean	alien		illness		
		*sense			cleanness	
		*scene				

SORT

ness   ean   *ense   ice
*seen-scene

TRANSFER

price   mean   meanness   dense

78

LETTERS

a i i o o u c c m m n n t

MAKE

at	cat/	moon	mount	commit	uncommon	communication
	act		count	common	mountain	
			comic	nation		
			comma	motion		
				action		
				amount		

*account
*caution/
*auction

SORT

com   tion   at   ount
Word relatives: common, uncommon

TRANSFER

chat   flat   bat   combat

LESSON 37

LETTERS

i o u y c m m n t

MAKE

mom	Tony	unity	county	community
Tom	tiny	minty	*mutiny	
nut	city	mount	commit	
cut	mint	count		
coy	unit			
toy				

SORT

com   y   ount   oy   ut

TRANSFER

joy   shut   strut   amount

LETTERS

e e i o o c h m n n p r s

This can be a two-day lesson, or pick and choose some words.

MAKE

hop	ship	chore	chrome	someone	microphone	comprehension
hip	chip	shore	choose	pension		
	chop	snore	cheers	erosion		
	shop	score	shrimp	compose		
	shoe	porch	sphere			
	echo	pooch	prison	composer		
	more	phone	person	scorpion		
	core	chose	poison	pioneers		
		choir	sermon			
			income			

SORT

com   sion   ch   sh   ph

ore   ip   op   on (person, sermon . . .)

Word relatives: compose, composer . . .

TRANSFER

trip   drop   store   common

LESSON 39

LETTERS

a a i o o u c g l n n r s t t

This can be a two-day lesson, or pick and choose some *words.*

MAKE

cut	clot	uncoil	closing	contrast	astronaut	congratulations
rot	slot	unclog	causing	constant	nocturnal	
	coil	artist	nursing	clotting	continual	
	clog	racist	unicorn	unstrung		
	unit	casual	cutting	organist	consultant	
		annual	rotting			
	union	caring	tourist			
			contain			
			consult			

SORT

con   un   uni   al   ist
ing (spelling changes)   ot

TRANSFER

not   knot   plotting   slingshot

82

LETTERS

e i o u c c c n n t t

MAKE

one	none	ounce	intent	content	*continue	Connecticut
	tone	unite		*conceit		
	cone	union		connect		
	tent	*tonic				
	cent	*tunic				
	unit					
	once					

SORT

con   uni   ent   one (two pronunciations)

TRANSFER

done   stone   phone   spent

LESSON 41

LETTERS

a i o o u c g n s t

MAKE

in	inn	stun	stung	cousin	*auction/	contagious
	tin	suit	sting	action	*caution	
	sun	song			suction	
	gun	sing				
		sung				

SORT

tion   in   ing   un   ung

in-inn

TRANSFER

spin   swing   lung   spun

LETTERS

e i o c n n n t t

MAKE

not	once/	notice	content	*innocent	continent
cot	cone				
ice	tone				
one	none				
	note				
	tote				
	tent				
	cent				
	nice				

SORT

con   one (two pronunciations)   ot   ote   ent
ice (two pronunciations)

TRANSFER

done   throne   consent   condone

LESSON 43

LETTERS

e i o u c n r s t

MAKE

corn	crust	nicest/	counter/	*corniest	countries
nose	count	insect	recount	counties	
nice	nurse	*insert			
rust	curse	nosier			
	cries	cousin			
	tries	*cruise			
	nicer				

SORT

ies (two pronunciations)   er   est   urse   ust

Word relatives: count, recount, counter . . .

Point out that the words ending in -ies ended in -y before they were changed.

TRANSFER

purse   trust   dust   dustier

LETTERS

e i o o c c d l r s

MAKE

ice	rice	loose	closed	*soldier	crocodiles
	dice	drool	closer		
	lice	slice	soccer		
	cool	rodeo	*oriole		
	rose	close	*circle		
	dose				
	lose				

SORT

c   ice   ose (three pronunciations)   ool

Word relatives: close, closed, closer

Point out two meanings and pronunciations for *close.*

TRANSFER

chose   those   price   school

LESSON 45

LETTERS

a e i o o c d n r s t

MAKE

no	act	crate/	dancer	tornado	*distance	*coordinates/
so		react	donate	cartoon	reaction	decorations
	date	actor	doctor	*senator	*creation	
		donor	indoor			
		dance	action			

SORT

or   tion   o   ate

Word relatives: act, react, reaction . . .

Point out that sometimes -or at the end of a word indicates a person.

TRANSFER

late   motion   potion   portion

LETTERS

a e o y c c d m r

MAKE

cry	army	adore	dreamy	*comrade	democracy
dry	code	decay	*comedy		
Roy	rode	decoy			
arm	road	ready			
	more	*mercy			
		dream			
		cream			

SORT

y (two pronunciations)   de   *com   ode   oy
road-rode

TRANSFER

shy   joy   deny   destroy

LESSON 47

LETTERS

e i o u c d n r s t t

This can be a two-day lesson, or pick and choose some *words.*

MAKE

out	tied	scent	cousin	outside	consider	destruction
tie	unit	disco	detour	distort	contrite	
	undo	outer	unrest	tourist	outcries	
	tour	trout	untied/	dentist	discount	
	rest	scout	united	student		
	test	snout	rodent	section	introduce	
	tent	under	outset	suction	reduction	
	sent			untried		
	cent			contest		

SORT

un   uni   tion   out   con   dis   ist   ent   est

sent-cent-scent

Word relatives: tour, tourist . . .

Point out that *un-* often signals an opposite relationship and that
uni- sometimes means "one" or "the same."

TRANSFER

conquest   consent   content   contentment

LESSON 48

LETTERS

a i o u d n r s s

MAKE

us	son	raid	drain	around	dinosaurs
do	sun	said	*radio	unsaid	
	aid	undo	*audio		
		rain	arson		
			*sinus		
			sound		
			round		

SORT

un   ound   aid   ain   sun-son
Word relatives: round, around . . .
Point out that *un-* often signals an opposite relationship.

TRANSFER

paid   unpaid   unchain   unsound

91

LESSON 49

LETTERS

i u c d g k l n s

MAKE

in	ink	sink	*slung	ducklings
		link	*slunk	
		lunk	*slink	
		luck	sling	
		duck	slick	
		dunk	clink	
		gunk	snuck	
		lick		
		sick		
		king		
		sing		
		sung		
		lung		

SORT

ick   uck   ink   unk   ing   ung

TRANSFER

brick   think   string   truck

LETTERS

e e i o c l n s t

MAKE

ten	nice	slice	select	enclose	selection/
tin	lice	elect	insect	*silence/	elections
ice			client	*license	
			notice	*stencil	
			listen/	section	
			enlist		

SORT

tion   en   ice (two pronunciations)

TRANSFER

price   twice   men   mention

LESSON 51

LETTERS

a e e i i c c l n r s t

MAKE

eel	reel	learn	screen	central	electric	electricians
	real	clean	circle	airline		
	seal	steal	*cereal	*elastic		
	teen	steel	center			
	seen					
	lean					
	earn					

SORT

eal eel, een ean (two spellings, one pronunciation)

real-reel   steal-steel

Word relatives: center, central . . .

TRANSFER

green   mean   heal   heel (check all in dictionary)

LETTERS

a e e h l n p s t

MAKE

eat	heel	eaten	please/	planets	elephants
eel	heal	phase	asleep		
	heat	steal			
	heap	steep			
	leap	sheep			
		sleep			
		sleet			
		steel			

SORT

ph   eal eel, eap eep, eat eet (Note two spelling patterns for all these rhymes.)

heel-heal   steal-steel

Word relatives: sleep, asleep; eat, eaten

TRANSFER

street   squeal   cheap   cheep (check all in dictionary)

LESSON 53

LETTERS

a e e e d d g n n r

MAKE

Ed	Ned	read/	greed	danger/	*degrade	*renegade	endangered
	red	dear	dread	garden	*grenade	*deranged	
		near	grade	endear			
		dead		enrage			
		deed		degree			
		need					

SORT

*de   en   ade   ed   eed   ead (*ead* is sometimes pronounced like *ed* and sometimes like *eed*.)
red-read

TRANSFER

bred   bread   bleed   bedspread (check all in dictionary)

LETTERS

a e i i u c h n s s t t

MAKE

ten	then	tenth	snatch	stitches	*scientist	enthusiastic
the	than	catch	snitch	*suitcase		
	thin	hatch	insect	*hesitant		
	that		itches			
	itch		inches			
	inch		stitch			

SORT

th   s/es   atch   itch
Word relatives: ten, tenth . . .

TRANSFER

scratch   scratches   switch   switches

LESSON 55

LETTERS

e e i o m n n n r t v

MAKE

over	never/	*meteor	*reinvent	environment
note	nerve	*motive	*overtime	
vote/	movie	remote		
veto	event	invent		
rent	voter			
vent	miner			
even	meter			
ever				

SORT

er   ote   ent

Word relatives: mine, miner . . .

TRANSFER

quote   wrote   sent   spent

LETTERS

a e i i g m n s t t

MAKE

sit	time	stain	timing	teasing	*instigate	estimating
set	gate	state/		tasting		
met	sane	taste		sitting		
	mane			setting		
	main			*imitate		
	gain			*imagine		

SORT

ing (spelling changes)   ate   it   et

ain ane (two spellings, one pronunciation)

main-mane

TRANSFER

split   splitting   betting   imagining

LESSON 57

LETTERS

a a e i o o n p r t v

MAKE

ant	rate	opera	proven	portion	*operation	evaporation
ate	rant	print	pirate	*private		
	pant	prove	option/	*protein		
	pint		potion			
	pair					
	pear					

SORT

tion   ate   ant

pair-pare

Word relatives: prove, proven

TRANSFER

grant   chant   state   gate

LETTERS

a e i u g h n s t x

MAKE

ate	taxi	exist	hating	exhaust	exhausting
six	gate	taxes/			
use/	hate	Texas			
sue	site	sixth			
tax	exit	sight			
		using/			
		suing			

SORT

ex   ing (spelling changes)   ate

eight-ate   site-sight

Word relatives: six, sixth; tax, taxes . . .

TRANSFER

date   dating   skate   skating

LESSON 59

LETTERS

a a e i o b f h l n s

MAKE

an   ban   bash   shelf   inhale   *abolish   fashionable
              lash   flash   banish
              fish   snail
              fail   alone
              bail   shone
              bale
              sale
              sail
              bone
              lone
              loan
              self

SORT

ash   ish   ale ail (two spellings, one pronunciation)   an   one
bail-bale   sale-sail   lone-loan

TRANSFER

cash   smash   vanish   Spanish

LETTERS

a e i f l s s t v

MAKE

eat	east	stale/	*fiesta	festivals
	fast	least	*siesta	
	fist	feast	itself	
	list			
	last			
	vast			
	vest			
	sale			
	sail			
	tail			
	tale			

SORT

ast ist east ale ail (two spellings, one pronunciation)
sail-sale   tail-tale

TRANSFER

beast   blast   pail pale (check in dictionary)

LESSON 61

LETTERS

a o o b f l l s t

MAKE

ball	aloft	*ballot	softball	footballs
tall	float			
toll	boats/			
tool	boast			
fool	boost/			
fast	boots			
last/	blast			
salt	stall			
solo	stool			
sofa				
oft				
loft				

SORT

all   ast   ool   oat
Word relatives: ball, softball, footballs

TRANSFER

mall   past   throat   pool

L E T T E R S

a i o c f n r s t

M A K E

an	ran	fist	faint	*casino	fractions
		cost	saint	*factor	
		corn	craft		
			first		
			facts		
			sonic		
			tonic		
			arson		
			coast		
			roast		
			acorn		
			scorn		

S O R T

ic   an   aint   oast   orn

T R A N S F E R

born   paint   panic   frantic

LESSON 63

LETTERS

eiifgghnnrt

MAKE

tire	ninth	fright	*inherit	frighten	frightening
hire	tiger	firing	freight		
fire	thief	hiring			
fine	grief	*ignite			
nine	eight				
	right				
	fight				

SORT

ing   ight   eight   ine   ire   ief
Word relatives: nine, ninth . . .

TRANSFER

weight   chief   shine   shining

LETTERS

a e o y g g h p r

MAKE

go	ago	rage	grope	*gopher	geography
	age	page/	grape		
		gape	*gorge		
		yoga	*opera		
		ahoy	graph		
		hero			
		gore			
		rope			
		hope			

SORT

a (ago, yoga)   ph   age   ape   ope

TRANSFER

scrape   stage   slope   scope

LESSON 65

LETTERS

e e o g m n n r s t v

MAKE

go	see	seen	stove	remove	monster	governments
		teen	grove	movers	segment	
		song	green	vetoes	governs	
		goes	greet	strong		
		veto				
		move				

SORT

ment   s/es   een   ong   ove (two pronunciations)

Word relatives: move, remove, movers . . .

TRANSFER

prove   drove   wrong   movement

LETTERS

a e i c d d g h l n n r

This can be a two-day lesson, or pick and choose some words.

MAKE

and	hide	heard	ranger	hearing	children	grandchildren
hid	care	dread	danger	landing		
	land	diner	hanger	dancing	grandchild	
	hang	dined	dinner	darling		
	dine	cared	danced	grannie		
	head	child	landed	earring		
	read	dance	ending			
	lead	anger/	caring			
	hard	range	harden			
	herd		hidden			
	hear					

SORT

ed   ing   en   er   and   ead (two pronunciations)

herd-heard

Word relatives: grandchild, grandchildren . . .

TRANSFER

bead   thread   hiding   grandstand

LESSON 67

LETTERS

a a e d f g h n r r s t

MAKE

gas	rage	draft	father	strange	*stagehand	grandfathers
age	raft	after		arrange		
		range		rafters		
		great/		gardens		
		grate		*transfer		
		stage				

SORT

aft   age   ange

great-grate

Word relatives: stage, stagehand; father, grandfathers

TRANSFER

page   cage   wages   crafts

LETTERS

a e o d g h m n r r s t

MAKE

one	done	groan	throne	another	grandmothers
	tone	other	dragon	armrest	
	game	horse	garden		
	name	stone	mother		
	same	drone			
	tame				
	moan				

SORT

ame   oan one (two pronunciations, two spellings)

TRANSFER

none   shame   lone loan (check in dictionary)

LESSON 69

LETTERS

e e e o u g h n r s

MAKE

go	rug	hour	house	enough	*surgeon	greenhouse
hug	goes	horse	hunger		
our	gone	shrug		*generous	
	hung	green			
	rung	rough			
	sung/				
	snug				
	shoe				
	huge				

SORT

g   ung   ug   ough   our-hour

TRANSFER

tough   lug   lung   strung

112

LETTERS

a i y c g m n s s t

MAKE

gas	gain	misty	*antics	gymnast	gymnastics
gym	sign	minty	sanity		
	mint	stain	stingy		
	mist	magic	*assign		
		manic			
		giant			
		nasty			

SORT

g   y   ic   ain

TRANSFER

rain   rainy   brainy   maintain

LESSON 71

LETTERS

a a e i c d d h n p p

MAKE

nap	chip	pinch	napped	chipped	handicapped
dip	dine	chain/	dipped	pinched	
	hide	China			
	pain	dined			
	pane	*panic			
	cane	panda			
	*ache	dance			
	acid				
	idea				
	inch				

SORT

ed (spelling changes)   c/ch   ain   ane   inch   ip
pain-pane

TRANSFER

cinch   ship   shipped   slipped

LETTERS

a e i i o b h n n r t

This can be a two-day lesson, or pick and choose some words.

MAKE

or	heir	ninth	Bertha	inhabit	baritone	hibernation
	herb	inner	orient	inherit		
ore	born	habit	throne	inertia		
oar	horn	orbit	hornet			
one	bear/	birth	obtain			
bit	bare	berth	retain/			
hit	bore		retina			
air	boar		intern			
	none		inborn			
	bone					
	tone					
	tore					
	nine					

SORT

in   it   one (two pronunciations)   ore oar (two spellings, one pronunciation)

air-heir   bear-bare   bore-boar   birth-berth   or-ore-oar

Word relatives: nine, ninth; in, inner

TRANSFER

done   stone   roar   shore (check in dictionary)

LESSON 73

LETTERS

a i o o u h m p p p s t

MAKE

out	pout	thump	*smooth	*shampoo	hippopotamus
	push	stump			
	pump	stamp			
		stomp			
		stoop			
		hoops			
		hoots/			
		shoot			
		shout			
		spout			
		mouth			
		south			
		*photo			

SORT

s/sh   oop   oot   out   outh   ump

TRANSFER

boots   troop   trout   trump

LETTERS

a i i g m m n r s t

MAKE

an	tan	gram	grain	margin	ramming	immigrants
	tin	grim	grant	rating		
	Tim	trim	grits	mating/	trimming	
	rim	grin	giant	taming	migrants	
	ram			timing		

SORT

ing (spelling changes)   g   am   an   im   in

TRANSFER

swim   swimming   plan   planning

LETTERS

e e e e i c d d n n n p

MAKE

end	iced	dined	pinned	deepened	independence
pen	died	ended	penned		
pin	need		needed	dependence	
die	deed		depend		
ice	deep		denied		
	dine		deepen		

SORT

ed (spelling changes)   de   eed   end
Word relatives: depend, dependence, independence

TRANSFER

greed   spend   defend   defended

LETTERS

e e i i d g n n r s t

MAKE

sing/	diner	dinner	stinger	desiring	inserting	ingredients
sign	enter	dining	grinned	entering		
grin	sting	desire		inserted		
dine		singer/		*redesign		
		signer		*ringside		
		*resign				
		*design				
		insert				

SORT

ed   er   ing

Word relatives: design, redesign; sing, singer . . .

TRANSFER

ring   fling   string   ringer

LETTERS

e i o c n p r s s t

MAKE

one	once	scent	nicest	inspect	*princess	inspectors
	nose	price	notice	nosiest		
	nice	coins	nosier	stepson		
	rent	nicer	insert	*protein		
	sent		insect	*process		
	cent					

SORT

in   c   er   est   ice (two pronunciations)   ent

cent-sent-scent

Word relatives: inspect, inspectors; nose, nosier . . .

TRANSFER

rice   twice   invent   indent

LETTERS

e e i i o c n n p r t t

MAKE

no	tent	entire	protest	*reception	*repetition	interception
	cent	entice	protect	*retention		
pro		encore	percent	*recipient		
	enter	center/		intercept		
		recent	Internet			
		recipe				

SORT

inter   re   en   pro   *tion   o   ent

Word relatives: intercept, interception

TRANSFER

repent   motion   promotion   protection

LETTERS

e e e e i c f n n r t

MAKE

in	inn	tree	fence	entire	retiree	*inference	interference
	fee	free	enter	entice	referee	interfere	
	tee	fire		recent			
		tire		*recite			
				retire			

SORT

inter   re   en   ee   ence   ire

in-inn

Word relatives: interfere, interference; retire, retiree

TRANSFER

three   rewire   require   sentence

LETTERS

e e i i n r s t v w

MAKE

new	view	write	entire	*reinvest	interviews
	west	wrist	invite		
	nest	renew	invent		
	rest		invest		
	tire		*invert		
	wire		*insert		
			viewer/		
			review		
			revise		

SORT

in   re   wr   est   ire

TRANSFER

infest   request   require   inspire

LETTERS

a i i i o n n s t t v

MAKE

go	inn	ants/	stain/	vision	station	invasion	invitations
so	tan	Stan	saint/		instant		
an			satin				
in			toast				
			visit				

SORT

tion sion o an

in-inn

TRANSFER

motion   lotion   notion   mansion (check all in dictionary)

LETTERS

e e i o k l m r s t

MAKE

like	slime	meteor/	*loiters	kilometers
Mike	smoke	remote	*omelets	
milk	stoke	*stereo		
silk	meter	strike		
slim		stroke		
time		liters		
lime				

SORT

ime   ilk   ike   oke

TRANSFER

prime   joke   choke   spike

LESSON 83

LETTERS

a e e i d d h k n r t

MAKE

hid	hard	knead	thread	*neither	kindhearted
	dark	*dread	darken	redhead	
	rank	drink	harden		
	rink	drank	hidden	darkened	
	head	thank	*either	hardened	
	dead	think			
	read	there			
	knit	their			
	knee				

SORT

kn   en   ed   ank   ink   ead (two pronunciations)

there-their

Word relatives: hard, harden, hardened

TRANSFER

plead   bead   bread   spread

126

LETTERS

a e i i b l r r s

MAKE

ear/	sale	*laser	*barrel	libraries
are	sail		*rabies	
air	rail			
ail	bail			
ale	bale			
	base			
	bare			
	rare			
	labs/			
	slab			

SORT

ail ale (two spellings, one pronunciation)

are (two pronunciations)

sail-sale   bail-bale

TRANSFER

trail   jail   snail   scale (check all in dictionary)

LESSON 85

LETTERS

a e e i u l r r t

MAKE

eat	tree	later	litter	trailer	literature
lie	late	treat	letter	retreat	
tie		trial/	turtle		
tea		trail	rattle		
tee		title			
		liter			

SORT

le   eat   ee   ie
tea-tee

TRANSFER

die   heat   beetle   steeple

LETTERS

a e u b c j k l m r s

MAKE

use	cure	brake/	*muscle	curable	lumberjacks
	sack	break	marble/	crumble	
	lack	baker	ramble		
	rack		rumble/		
	back		lumber		
	buck		usable		
	luck				
	*muck				
	bark				
	lark				
	bake				

SORT

able   le   ark   ack   uck
break-brake
Word relatives: bake, baker; lumber, lumberjacks

TRANSFER

struck   buckle   chuckle   packable

LESSON 87

LETTERS

a a e i g m n s z

MAKE

man	sage	amaze	manage	amazing	magazines
men	zing	image		*amnesia	
gem	sing/				
nag	sign				
zag	size				
zig	gaze				
age	maze				

SORT

g   ag   age (two pronunciations)   aze

Word relatives: amaze, amazing

TRANSFER

blaze   cage   bag   baggage

LETTERS

a a e i c h m m s t t

MAKE

mat	mats	chest	static	matches	mathematics
	math	steam/	stitch		
	mash	teams	itches	attaches	
	cash	match	attach		
	itch	attic			
	team				
	test				

SORT

s/es   ic   ash   itch   eam   est
Word relatives: match, matches . . .

TRANSFER

west   cream   switch   switches

LETTERS

a e i u g m n r s

MAKE

rug	sure	amuse	margin	amusing	*geraniums
mug/	germ	argue	manger	erasing	measuring
gum		using/	*mirage		
gem		suing	*genius		
use/			insure		
sue					

SORT

sure   ing   g   ue   ug

TRANSFER

plug   shrug   glue   gluing

LETTERS

eeioooglmrsstt

This can be a two-day lesson, or pick and choose some words.

MAKE

go	time	gloom	settle	moistest	tortoises	meteorologists
	tire	igloo	sitter	gloomier	motorists	
sit	goes	timer	gooier	roomiest	stormiest	
	solo	moist		timeless	gloomiest	
	loot	motto	gooiest	tireless	mistletoe	
	root	motor	goriest	rootless		
	room	storm	mottoes	termites		
			looters	settlers		
			soloist	tortoise		
			legroom			
			moister			

SORT

less   er/est   s/es   ist   er   oom   oot
Word relatives: motor, motorists . . .

TRANSFER

doom   bloom   shoot   shooter

LESSON 91

LETTERS

e e i i l l m m r s t

MAKE

sell	slime/	resell/	*trellis	smellier	millimeters
tell	miles/	seller	*sterile		
till	smile		sillier		
mill	still		slimier		
time	smell				
tile					
mile/					
lime					

SORT

er   ell   ill   ile   ime

Word relatives: slime, slimier; sell, resell, seller . . .

TRANSFER

chill   chillier   grime   grimier

LETTERS

a e e i u k l m w

MAKE

we	wee	weak/	alike	*leukemia	Milwaukee
		wake			
		make			
		lake/			
		leak			
		leek			
		week			
		*meek			
		meal/			
		male			
		mail			
		mile			
		Mike			
		like			

SORT

eak eek (two spellings, one pronunciation)   ake   ike
we-wee   weak-week   mail-male   leak-leek

TRANSFER

peak   peek   creek   creak (check all in dictionary)

LETTERS

a e i o m n n s t

MAKE

in	tin	none	stain	insane	*nominate	Minnesota
	ten	tone/	stone	inmate		
	ate	note		tennis		
	one	sane				
		mane/				
		name				
		same				
		tame/				
		mate				
		main				

SORT

in   ine   one (two pronunciations)   ame
ane ain (two spellings, one pronunciation)
main-mane

TRANSFER

phone   done   spine   incline

LESSON 94

LETTERS

e i o o u d d m n r s s t

This can be a two-day lesson, or pick and choose some words.

MAKE

use	mood	miner	sunrise	monstrous	misunderstood
sun	mess	minor	monster	roominess	
mud	moss	minus	stories	moodiness	
	toss	dress	studies	muddiness	
	tour	dries	minuses		
	room		tourism	understood	
	riot	misuse	serious		
	mine	sunset	riotous		
			enormous		

SORT

mis ous ness s/es ess oss
miner-minor
Word relatives: tour, tourism; mine, miner . . .

TRANSFER

less   bless   cross   crossness

LESSON 95

LETTERS

i i o b c d g k m n r s

MAKE

ink	sink	smock	kingdom	songbird	mockingbirds
	mink	brick			
	rink	brisk			
	risk	brink			
	king	drink			
	sick	bingo			
	sock				
	rock				
	dock				
	bird				

SORT

ink   ick   ock
Word relatives: king, kingdom

TRANSFER

stick   stink   shrink   shock

LETTERS

e i o o u m q s s t

MAKE

sit	some	quite/	tissue	misquote	mosquitoes
use/	toes	quiet	misuse		
sue	omit	quest			
sum	emit	quote			
	quit	mouse			
		moose			
		issue			

SORT

mis   qu   it   ue

sum–some

Word relatives: use, misuse; quote, misquote

TRANSFER

split   cue   misfit   miscue

LESSON 97

LETTERS

i i u y g l l m n p t

MAKE

my	ply	glum	lumpy	typing	lumpily	guiltily	multiplying
	ump	plum	minty	glumly		multiply	
	gum	pity	guilt				
		puny					
		ugly					
		tiny					
		lily					
		mint					
		lump					

SORT

y (two pronunciations)   ly (spelling changes)   um   ump
Word relatives: glum, glumly . . .

TRANSFER

strum   grump   grumpy   grumpily

LETTERS

e e i y m r s s t

MAKE

I	eye	stem	misty	misery	messier	mysteries
	try	mess	messy	sister/		
	sty	miss	tries	resist		
		mist	sties	*series		
		miser		*system		

SORT

y (two pronunciations)

y-i   I-eye

TRANSFER

cry   cries   dry   driest

LESSON 99

LETTERS

e i o o o b d g h h n r

MAKE

hi	high	ridge	bridge	ignored	neighborhood
	hire	bored	higher	*honored	
	bore	*honor	behind		
	gore	rodeo	*region/		
	bind	grind	ignore		
	ride	bride			

SORT

ed   ide   idge   ind   ore

hi-high   hire-higher

Word relatives: high, higher . . .

TRANSFER

glide   glided   mind   beside

LETTERS

a e e n p p r s s w

MAKE

are/	wrap/	renew	seesaw	snapper	newspapers
ear	warp	*swear	*answer		
saw	warn	spear			
paw	wars	paper			
raw	were				
rap	wren				
	near				
	pear				
	wear				
	snap				
	news				

SORT

ap   aw   ear (two pronunciations)   wr

rap-wrap   wars-warp-warn

Word relatives: news, renew; paper, newspapers

TRANSFER

warm   wart   year   bear

LESSON 101

LETTERS

iiounnrtt

MAKE

out	riot	trout	tuition	nutrition
not	unit	union		
nut	into			
rut	noun			
rot	ruin			
	tour			
	trot			

SORT

tion   ot   ut   out

TRANSFER

scout   shot   shut   shout

144

LETTERS

e e i o u d f l r s t

This can be a two-day lesson, or pick and choose some *words.*

MAKE

us	use	tied/	filed/	refuse	defrost	outfield	outfielders
	old	tide	field	retold	loudest		
	oil	told	slide	refold	outside		
	tie	fold	older	relief			
		foul	outer	result			
		foil	reset	oldest			
		toil	reuse	louder			
		soil		forest/			
		loud		foster			
		ride		defuse			
		side		desire			
		tile		detour			
		file		desert			

SORT

out   de   re   er/est   use   old   ild   ile   ide   oil
tied/tide
Word relatives: field, outfield, outfielders . . .

TRANSFER

scold   coil   recoil   amuse

LESSON 103

LETTERS

a e e i u c d l n p p r r

This can be a two-day lesson, or pick and choose some words.

MAKE

rip	cruel	purple	clapped	audience	perpendicular
lap	pedal	ripple	replace		
	rural	nipple	cripple		
clap	repel	candle	prepare		
race	panel/	cradle	prepaid		
pace	plane	curdle	preplan		
duel	plain	cereal	pelican		
	place	denial			
	raced	pencil			
	pupil	parcel			
	peril	placed			
	peace	ripped			
	piece	lapped			
	uncle				

SORT

pre___ed (spelling changes)   al   el   le   il   ap   ace
peace-piece   plane-plain
Word relatives: rip, ripped . . .

TRANSFER

trap   trapped   trace   traced

LETTERS

a a e i i d h h l l p p

MAKE

Ed	led	pill	plead/	*appeal	*applied	Philadelphia
	all	hill	pedal			
	ill	hall	ahead			
		hail	apple			
		pail				
		pale				
		hale				
		idea				
		head				
		lead				

SORT

ead (two pronunciations)　all　ill　ale ail (two spellings, one pronunciation)

hail-hale　pail-pale　led-lead

TRANSFER

spread　thread　bale-bail (check in dictionary)

LESSON 105

LETTERS

e i o o y h h n p s s s t t

This can be a two-day lesson, or pick and choose some words.

MAKE

spy	pony	noise	snoopy	honesty	photosynthesis
shy	spot	noisy	ponies	typhoon	
	nose	shine	shiest	stepson	
	nosy	shiny	spotty	hostess	
	type	stone	typist	shyness	
	host	stony	tiptoe		
		photo	python	phoniest	
		phone	honest	hypnosis	
		phony			
		spies		hypnotist	
		snoop			
				hypothesis	

SORT

ph   y   y-ies, iest   ist   one

Word relatives: shy, shiest, shyness . . .

TRANSFER

spry   throne   cyclone   cyclist

LETTERS

i u b g h p r s t t

MAKE

sir	stir	spurt	bright	*upright	Pittsburgh
	rust	shirt		*uptight	
	gust	brush			
	bust	sight			
	bush	right			
	push	tight			
	rush	trust			
	gush				
	hurt				

SORT

ight   ush (two pronunciations)   ust   urt
Word relatives: tight, uptight . . .

TRANSFER

crush   flight   crust   blurt

LESSON 107

LETTERS

a e i o u m n n p

MAKE

in	pan/	nine	pneumonia
an	nap	mine	
	nip/	pine	
	pin	pane	
	pen	pain	
	men	main	
	man	mane/	
	map/	mean	
	Pam	moan	
		open	
		upon	

SORT

an   ap   ane   ain   en   in   ine

pain-pane   main-mane

TRANSFER

happen   napkin   insane   maintain (check in dictionary)

LETTERS

a e i i o n p s s t t

MAKE

tan	span	Spain	ponies	stepson	petition	poinsettias
pan	sane	stain	pities	pianist		
	pane	point	season			
	pain	piano	siesta			
			tiptoe			
			teapot			

SORT

ain ane (two spellings, one pronunciation)   an

pain-pane

Word relatives: piano, pianist

TRANSFER

crane   sprain   plain   plane (check all in dictionary)

LESSON 109

LETTERS

a o u l l n p s t t

MAKE

sun	aunt	slant	*postal	pollutants
son	pant	plant		
out	past	spout		
ant	last	stout		
	pout	snout		
	poll	pants		
	toll	*total		
	also			
	upon			

SORT

ant   ast   oll   out
sun-son

TRANSFER

stroll   blast   sprout   chant

LETTERS

a e i i i o c n p p r t t

MAKE

not	topic	tropic	caption	petition	reappoint	precipitation
pot	tonic	poetic	protect	creation	patriotic	
	panic	action	protein	traction		
poet	attic		propane	reaction		
			patriot			
			apricot			

SORT

pro   re   tion   ic   ot

Word relatives: poet, poetic . . .

TRANSFER

plot   picnic   fiction   friction

LESSON 111

LETTERS

e e i d n p r s s t

This can be a two-day lesson, or pick and choose some *words.*

MAKE

end	send	spend	resist	dessert	ripeness	presidents
	sent	spent	resent	preside	dispense	
	dent	dress	reside	pretend	disperse	
	side	press	entire	present/	resident	
	peer	pride/	desert	serpent	sidestep	
	pier	pried		depress		
		tried/		redness	tiredness	
		tired				

SORT

dis   pre   re   ness   ess   end   ent   ide

pride-pried   peer-pier

Word relatives: preside, presidents; side, sidestep . . .

TRANSFER

distress   wide   wideness   beside

LETTERS

i o o y c g h l p s s t

MAKE

pool	ghost	school	ghostly	psychologist
loop	pilot	cohost	copilot	
hoop	stoop	gossip	soloist	
solo	stool	costly		
cost				
lost				
post				
host				

SORT

co   ist   ly   ool   oop

ost (two pronunciations)

Word relatives: cost, costly . . .

TRANSFER

scoop   frost   most   mostly

LETTERS

a a e e k l n r s s t t

This can be a two-day lesson, or pick and choose some words.

MAKE

ate/	neat	steel	street	anteater	alertness	rattlesnakes
eat	seat	steal		translate	alternate	
	late	stank		lateness		
	rate	ankle		realness		
	rank	treat				
	sank	sneak/				
	tank	snake				
	lake/	skate				
	leak	sleet				
	teak	skeet				
	teal	alert/				
	seal	alter				
	real					
	reel					

SORT

ness   ank   ate   ake   eak   eat   eal   eel   eet

real-reel   steel-steal

Word relatives: snake, rattlesnakes; eat, anteater . . .

TRANSFER

prank   flake   weak   weakness

L·E·T·T·E·R·S

a e e c g l n r s t

This can be a two-day lesson, or pick and choose some words.

M·A·K·E

lean	later	create	leanest	cleanest	rectangles
late	large	relate	largest	sergeant	
	steal	resale	enlarge	strangle	
	steel	recent/	reenact		
	clean	center	neglect		
	eagle	castle	central		
	easel	gentle	eternal		
	angel/	cereal	general		
	angle	enrage	elegant		
	react	senate	cleaner		
	enact	leaner			
	crate				

S·O·R·T

re   en   al/el/le   er/est   ate

steel-steal

Word relatives: angle, rectangles; center, central . . .

T·R·A·N·S·F·E·R

date   gate   state   rebate

LESSON 115

LETTERS

e e e f h m n r r s s t

MAKE

see	free	these	reenter	freshmen	refreshments
fee	tree	three	refresh	*semester	
	nest	enter			
	rest	fresh		*freshener	
	rent	reset			
	sent	refer			
	them				
	then	resent			

SORT

re   ent   est   ee

Word relatives: fresh, freshmen, refresh . . .

TRANSFER

spree   spent   repent   request

LETTERS

a e e i l r s t v

MAKE

set	seal	steal	relive	*several	*versatile/
	real	trial	reseal		relatives
		rival	reveal		
		vital	revise		
		easel	travel		
		reset			

SORT

re   al   el   eal

TRANSFER

deal   squeal   repeal   rebel

LESSON 117

LETTERS

a a e i o l n r t x

MAKE

ax	tax	oxen	alone	*loiter	*elation	relation	relaxation
ox	lax	exit	alert/				
		taxi	alter				
		tone	altar				
		lone	relax				
		loan	extra				
		roan	*liter				

SORT

tion ex ax one oan (two spellings, one pronunciation)

loan-lone alter-altar

Word relatives: relax, relaxation; ox, oxen; lone, alone

TRANSFER

wax zone phone moan (check in dictionary)

LETTERS

e e o p r r r s t

MAKE

see	tree	sport	terror	restore	reporters
	rest	spree	stereo		
	pest	error	poster		
	rose		pester		
	pose		report		
	post		resort		
	port				
	sort				

SORT

re   ee   est   ose   ort
Word relatives: port, report, reporters . . .

TRANSFER

those   quest   request   retest

LETTERS

e e i o b l n p r s s

MAKE

lion	bless	reopen	replies	boneless	responsible
bone	sense	relies	lioness	ripeness	
ripe	rebel			sensible	
boss				possible	
loss				response	
less					

SORT

ible   re   ess   oss

Word relatives: lion, lioness; sense, sensible . . .

TRANSFER

cross   across   stress   recess

LETTERS

e i o o c h n r r s

MAKE

one	once	chore	choose	*cornier	*schooner	rhinoceros
	nice	shore	inches	onshore		
	inch	snore	riches	*erosion		
	rich	choir	heroic			
	hero	chose	enrich			
	echo		corner			
	core					

SORT

c/ch (four sounds)   s/es   ore
Word relatives: hero, heroic; shore, onshore . . .

TRANSFER

score   adore   before   enriches

LESSON 121

LETTERS

e i i c n s s t t

MAKE

ice	nice	scent	insect	iciness	scientists
	tent	since	insist	tiniest	
	test		nicest		
	nest/		cities/		
	sent		iciest		
	cent				

SORT

est (spelling changes)   ent   ice

sent-cent-scent

Word relatives: ice, iciest, iciness . . .

TRANSFER

spent   spice   spiciest   spiciness

LETTERS

a e o o b c d r r s

MAKE

bar	soar	scare	scared/	*boarder	scoreboard
	sore	board	*sacred	scarred	
	core	bored	record		
	bore	score	barred		
	boar	adore	*border		
	roar	rodeo			
	scar				

SORT

ed (spelling changes)   oar   ore

soar-sore   bore-boar   board-bored   border-boarder

Word relatives: board, boarder . . .

TRANSFER

star   starred   adored   scored

LESSON 123

LETTERS

a e i i f l m n s s

MAKE

name	smile/	aliens	*inflame	*families	semifinals
fame	slime	Lassie	*missile		
same	snail				
sale	flame				
male	final				
mail					
sail					
nail					
fail					
file					
mile					

SORT

ame   ale   ail   ile (two pronunciations)

sale-sail   male-mail

Word relatives: flame, inflame

TRANSFER

frame   became   while   reptile

LETTERS

a a e i o l n n s s t

MAKE

lies	atlas	stolen	atlases	seasonal	sensational
ties	*alias	listen/	*aliases	national	
	nasal	tinsel		toenails	
	steal	tassel			
	stole	enlist		sensation	
		entail			
		nation			
		season			

SORT

tion   en   al   el   s/es

Word relatives: season, seasonal . . .

TRANSFER

mention   motion   option   optional

LETTERS

a a e i o b d g k n r s t

This can be a two-day lesson, or pick and choose some words.

MAKE

ate	gait	store	stroke	bargain	skateboarding
age	bait	skate	donate	against	
ask	rain	stage	bandit	sandbag	
oak	rank	stain	basket	senator	
	sank	brain	ignore	storage	
soak	task	drain		bandage	
rage	bore	again			
rate	boar	orbit		sabotage	
date	soar	broke		drainage	
gate	sore	stoke			

SORT

ain age ank ask ate ait oar ore oak oke
(Note two pronunciations for *ain, age* and two spelling patterns for
rhymes *ate, ait; oar, ore; oak, oke.*)
bore-boar soar-sore gait-gate
Word relatives: store, storage . . .

TRANSFER

page package maintain captain

LETTERS

o o m n r s s t w

MAKE

to	two	snow	worst	snowstorm
	too	stow	motor	
	moo	soon	swoon	
	mow	moon	storm	
	row	worm		
	tow			
	sow			
	now			

SORT

ow (two pronunciations)   oon

to-too-two

Word relatives: snow, storm, snowstorm

TRANSFER

chow   flow   throw   below

LESSON 127

LETTERS

a a e u c c l p r s t

MAKE

us	use/	true	super	clause	capture	spectacular
	sue	cute	atlas	cactus	pasture	
	cue	plus	pause	accept		
		trap	cause	accuse	*accurate	
		slap		salute		

SORT

ture   ause   ap   ue   us   ute   use
acc-accept, accuse, accurate

TRANSFER

strap   rapture   because   applause

LETTERS

a i u b c g n r s t t

MAKE

bat	stub	stung	guitar	batting	*curtains	subtracting
cut	rang	stunt	string	cutting		
rub	rung	sting	strung			
sub	ring	scrub	*strict			
	sing	scuba	strain			
	sang		*static			
	sung		*tragic			

SORT

ing (spelling changes)   ang   ing   ung   ub
Word relatives: sing, sang, sung . . .

TRANSFER

hang   hung   club   clubbing

LESSON 129

LETTERS

a a e e m m s t t

MAKE

at	ate/	seat/	taste/	estate	teammates
	eat	east	state		
	tea	team/	steam		
	tee	tame/			
	see	mate/			
	sea	meat			
		meet			
		same			

SORT

ame   ate   eat   eam

see-sea   tea-tee   meat-meet

Word relatives: team, mate, teammates

TRANSFER

cheat   treat   retreat   repeat

LETTERS

e e e o c l p s s t

MAKE

toes	slope	closet	steeple	telescopes
toss	elope	select		
loss	sleet			
lots	sleep			
lost	steep			
cost	slept			
post/				
spot/				
stop				
cope				

SORT

eep   ope   oss   ost (two pronunciations)
Word relatives: sleep, slept

TRANSFER

keep   kept   creep   crept

LETTERS

a o u d h n s s t

MAKE

and	hunt	*haunt	donuts	*handouts	thousands
out	hand	snout			
not	sand	shout/			
hot	shut	south			
hut	shot	sound			
nut	aunt	hound			
		stand			

SORT

sh   and   out   ot   ut   ound

TRANSFER

scout   found   rebound   grandstand

LETTERS

e o o u b h h r s t t

MAKE

our	hour	brush	thrust	brushes	*hothouse	toothbrushes
	*hobo	tours	robust	*booster		
	rust	usher	outset			
	rush	trust	*hoboes			
	hush		horses			
	bush		rushes			
			bushes			

SORT

s/es   ush (two pronunciations)   ust

our-hour

Word relatives: rush, rushes . . .

TRANSFER

push   pushes   rush   rushes

LETTERS

a e o u m n n r s t t

MAKE

set	meet	tuner	outran	*stature	ornament	tournaments
met	meat	tumor	outset	toaster	outsmart	
	sore	tutor	nature	monster		
	soar	toast	mature	senator		
	tune			*torment		

SORT

er   or   ment   ture   out   et

meet-meat   sore-soar

Word relatives: tune, tuner . . .

TRANSFER

outset   outlet   ferment   mixture

LETTERS

a i i o d n r s t t

MAKE

ant	sand	radio	strand	distant	*antiriot	traditions
and	road	*ratio	raisin	station		
	toad	toast				
	riot/	roast				
	trio	stand				

SORT

and   oad   oast

Word relatives: riot, antiriot

TRANSFER

coast   load   grand   grandstand

177

LETTERS

a e i g l n r s t

MAKE

nail	stale	tangle	*gristle	*strangle	triangles
rail	trial/	tingle			
tail	trail	tinsel			
tale	giant	rental			
	alien	signal			
	snail	single			
	angel/				
	angle				

SORT

al/le/el (three spellings, one pronunciation)   ale   ail

tail-tale

TRANSFER

bail bale   mail male

LETTERS

i o o u u c c n n s s

MAKE

on	con	noun	coins	onions	cousins	unconscious
	son	noon	sinus	unions/		
	sun	soon	sonic	*unison	conscious	
		cuss	onion			
		coin			*concussion	

SORT

con   uni   on (two pronunciations)   oon
son-sun

TRANSFER

contest   uniform   bonbons   monsoon

LETTERS

e o u d d g n r s

MAKE

do	due	send	surge	*drudge	*surgeon	underdogs
end	undo	under	ground	undergo	
	redo	sound	sudden	rounded	
	rude	round			
	dude	nudge			
	urge				

SORT

under   ound   ude   udge   urge

do-due

Word relatives: do, undo, redo . . .

TRANSFER

fudge   purge   hound   underground

LETTERS

e e i o u u d d h n n r r s

This can be a two-day lesson, or pick and choose some words.

MAKE

red	done	under	hidden	desired	underside	undernourished
run	hide	rider	redden	shunned	underdone	
sun	ride	riser	insure	hundred	nourished	
use	rise	rerun	ensure	hideous		
	user/	order	endure	reunion	surrounded	
	sure	union	runner			
	shun	shred	desire	disorder		
				shredder		

SORT

under   re   ed   er   en   un

Word relatives: shred, shredder (spelling changes) . . .

TRANSFER

stun   stunned   gun   gunner

LESSON 139

LETTERS

e e o u y l m m n n p t

MAKE

my	ply	melt	nylon	plenty	*monument	unemployment
	toy	pelt	penny	employ		
	yet	pony	money	moment	employment	
	pet	only	empty			
	met	type	enemy			
			lumpy			

SORT

ment   y (two pronunciations)   oy   et   elt
Word relatives: employ, employment, unemployment

TRANSFER

enjoy   enjoyment   payment   shipment

LETTERS

a e o u u f n n r t t

MAKE

fat	four	often	rotten	turnout	fortunate	unfortunate
rot	true		fatten	fortune		
not	tune		nonfat			
out	dune		future			
for			nature			
			untrue			
			outrun			

SORT

un   ture   en (spelling changes)   ot   une
for-four
Word relatives: fat, fatten, nonfat . . .

TRANSFER

got   gotten   mixture   capture

LESSON 141

LETTERS

a e e i u b c d l n p r t

This can be a two-day lesson, or pick and choose some words.

MAKE

act	crude	unpaid	decline	prudence	unpredictable
cut	prude	unreal	unclear	patience	
	decal	unable	include	audience	
cure	enact	entire	intrude	credible	
rude	uncle	entice	curable		
		endure	pretend	unrelated	
		endear	predict	endurable	
		precut	prudent		
		edible			
		derail			
		detail			
		detain			
		debate			
		depart			
		decent			

SORT

un   pre   de   en   ence   able   ible   ude
Word relatives: prudent, prudence . . .

TRANSFER

enter   delude   prepaid   unendurable

LETTERS

a a i o u y c f n r s s t t

This can be a two-day lesson, or pick and choose some words.

MAKE

nut	sour	unity	unfair	tourist	raincoat	unsatisfactory
art	four	unify	static	outcast	fraction	
our	your	rainy	outfit	factory	traction	
	tour	nutty	outran	satisfy		
	rain	fussy	outcry	caution/	fantastic	
	fuss	attic	artist	auction	astronaut	
	unit	scour		station		
		unfit		frantic	stationary	
					satisfactory	

SORT

y (two pronunciations)   out   un   uni   tion
ist   ic   our (three pronunciations)
Word relatives: satisfy, satisfactory . . .

TRANSFER

unicorn   fiction   friction   typist

LETTERS

euuccflnsss

MAKE

fun	self	uncle	unless	success	unsuccessful
sun	less		useful		
use/	fuss			successful	
sue	fuse				
cue	clue				
elf	fuel				

SORT

ful   elf   un   use   ue

Word relatives: use, useful . . .

TRANSFER

true   untrue   useless   clueless

LETTERS

a a i i o c c n n t v

MAKE

on	inn	into	tonic	cannot	contain	vacation	vaccination
in	Ann	antic	*vacant	*convict	*aviation		
	ant/	civic	action				
	tan		nation				
	van						
	can						
	con						
	act						

SORT

tion   con   ic   an   on
in-inn   can-cannot

TRANSFER

sonic   manic   friction   conviction

LESSON 145

LETTERS

a a e e i g n r s t v

This can be a two-day lesson, or pick and choose some *words.*

MAKE

see	give	reign	invent	average	sergeant	vegetarians
sea	save	great/	invest	against	trainees	
	rave	grate	invert	teasing	starving	
	rage	tease	insert	serving	negative	
	vine/	serve	strive	veteran	navigate	
	vein	train	native	vinegar		
	vain	again	enrage	vagrant		
	vane		starve	servant		
	rain		raving			
	rein		saving			
			savage			
			ravage			

SORT

in   ing (spelling changes)   age (two pronunciations)
ive (two pronunciations)
see-sea   great-grate   vein-vain-vane   rain-rein-reign
Word relatives: serve, servant . . .

TRANSFER

drive   driving   raging   image

188

LETTERS

a a e e i i n n r r t v

MAKE

rent	never/	invent	retrain/	*retainer	veterinarian
vent	nerve	invite	trainer		
rain	train	entire	*trainee		
ever	event	retire	*terrain		
		retain	veteran		

SORT

in   re   ain   ent

Word relatives: train, trainer, trainee, retrain . . .

TRANSFER

indent   resent   remain   regain

LESSON 147

LETTERS

a a o u y b c l r v

MAKE

by	buy	crab	curly	cavalry	vocabulary
	boa	club	cobra		
	rob	ruby/	royal		
	rub	bury	labor		
	cub	curb	Carol/		
	cob	curl	coral		
	cab				

SORT

ab   ob   ub   by-buy

Word relatives: curl, curly

TRANSFER

shrub   snob   grab   grub

LETTERS

a e o o c l n s v

MAKE

one	once/	slave/	*saloon	volcano	volcanoes
	cone	salve	cloves		
	lone	solve/	*alcove		
	soon	loves			
	loon	alone			
	love	ocean			
	cove	canoe			
	save	*salon			

SORT

ave   one   oon   ove (two pronunciations)

Word relatives: volcano, volcanoes; one, once . . .

TRANSFER

brave   stove   stone   spoon

LESSON 149

LETTERS

a e o y b l l l l s v

MAKE

sob	slob	above	valley	lovable	solvable	volleyballs
lob	ball	solve	*volley/		*syllable	
	bell	belly	lovely			
	sell	alley				
	yell					
	ally					
	love					

SORT

able   ell   ob

Word relatives: love, lovely, lovable; volley, volleyballs . . .

TRANSFER

smell   snob   throb   hobnob

LETTERS

e e i d l n r s s w

MAKE

end	wind	weird	slender	wildness	weirdness	wilderness
red	wild		winless	*idleness		
wed/	wire		endless	*dewiness		
dew	lend		redness	wireless		
win	*idle		windless			

SORT

less ness ed end

Word relatives: wild, wildness, wilderness . . .

TRANSFER

shred trend trendiness slenderness

PATTERNS INDEX

▪ Prefixes, Suffixes, Endings ▪

able	lumberjacks unpredictable volleyballs
al (spinal, petal)	calculators caterpillars celebrating congratulations perpendicular rectangles relatives sensational triangles
co (coauthor)	psychologist
com	communication community comprehension democracy
con	congratulations Connecticut continent destruction unconscious vaccination
de	democracy endangered independence outfielders unpredictable
dis	destruction presidents
ed	amendments grandchildren handicapped independence ingredients kindhearted neighborhood perpendicular scoreboard undernourished
el (panel)	caterpillars celebrating perpendicular rectangles relatives sensational triangles
en (eaten, smarten)	grandchildren kindhearted undernourished unfortunate
en (enrage, entire)	elections endangered interception interference rectangles sensational undernourished unpredictable
er (painter, sister)	bullfighter environment grandchildren ingredients meteorologists tournaments undernourished
er/est	centipedes countries inspectors meteorologists millimeters outfielders rectangles
ex (extra, expose)	exhausting relaxation
ful	cauliflower unsuccessful
ible	responsible unpredictable

ic (critic)	antibiotics fractions gymnastics mathematics precipitation unsatisfactory vaccination
il (pencil)	perpendicular
in (insane, inlet)	hibernation inspectors interviews Minnesota vegetarians veterinarian
ing	celebrating congratulations estimating exhausting frightening grandchildren immigrants ingredients measuring subtracting vegetarians
inter	interception interference
ist (realist)	congratulations destruction meteorologists photosynthesis psychologist unsatisfactory
le (little)	caterpillars celebrating literature lumberjacks perpendicular rectangles triangles
less	carelessness meteorologists wilderness
ly (nicely)	multiplying psychologist
ment	governments tournaments unemployment
mis	misunderstood mosquitoes
ness	carelessness cleanliness misunderstood presidents rattlesnakes wilderness
or (inspector, motor)	decorations tournaments
ous	adventurous misunderstood
out (outlive)	destruction tournaments outfielders unsatisfactory
pre (preteen, predict)	perpendicular presidents unpredictable
pro (program, process)	interception precipitation
re	barometers cauliflower celebrating cheerleaders interception interference interviews outfielders precipitation presidents rectangles refreshments relatives reporters responsible undernourished veterinarian
s/es	cholesterol enthusiastic governments mathematics meteorologists misunderstood rhinoceros sensational toothbrushes

sion	comprehension invitations
sure	measuring
tion	antibiotics communication contagious decorations destruction elections evaporation interception invitations nutrition precipitation relaxation sensational unsatisfactory vaccination
ture	spectacular tournaments unfortunate
un	congratulations destruction dinosaurs unfortunate unpredictable unsatisfactory
under	underdogs undernourished
uni	congratulations Connecticut destruction unconscious unsatisfactory
y (fly, fishy, yes)	biography birthdays community democracy multiplying photosynthesis unemployment
y (rainy)	democracy gymnastics multiplying mysteries photosynthesis unsatisfactory
y-ies, ied, ier, iest	anniversary countries mysteries photosynthesis

■ Digraphs, Consonants ■

c (cat, city)	candidates crocodiles handicapped inspectors rhinoceros
ch (chop, machine, echo)	characters comprehension handicapped rhinoceros
g (girl, gym)	greenhouse gymnastics immigrants magazines measuring
kn	kindhearted
ph	biography comprehension elephants geography photosynthesis
qu	mosquitoes
sh	comprehension hippopotamus thousands
th	enthusiastic
wr	interviews newspapers

■ Homophones ■

air-heir	hibernation
alter-altar	relaxation
ate-eight	exhausting
bale-bail	beautiful fashionable libraries
be-bee	barometers
bear-bare	hibernation
birth-berth	hibernation
boarder-border	scoreboard
bore-boar	hibernation scoreboard skateboarding
bored-board	scoreboard
break-brake	breakthroughs lumberjacks
by-buy	vocabulary
close-clothes	cholesterol
deer-dear	cheerleaders
do-due	underdogs
eye-I	mysteries
fare-fair	cauliflower
for-four	unfortunate
gait-gate	skateboarding
great-grate	grandfathers vegetarians
hail-hale	Philadelphia
heal-heel	cheerleaders elephants
herd-heard	cheerleaders grandchildren
hi-high	neighborhood
higher-hire	neighborhood
horse-hoarse	breakthroughs
in-inn	contagious interference invitations vaccination
leak-leek	Milwaukee
led-lead	Philadelphia
loan-lone	fashionable relaxation
mail-male	Milwaukee semifinals
main-mane	estimating Minnesota pneumonia
meat-meet	amendments teammates tournaments

miner-minor	misunderstood
or-ore-oar	bookstore hibernation
our-hour	greenhouse toothbrushes
pail-pale	Philadelphia
pair-pear	evaporation
pane-pain	handicapped pneumonia poinsettias
peace-piece	perpendicular
peer-pier	presidents
plane-plain	perpendicular
pride-pried	presidents
rain-rein	anniversary carnivores
rain-rein-reign	vegetarians
real-reel	cheerleaders electricians rattlesnakes
red-read	endangered
road-rode	democracy
roam-Rome	barometers
roll-role	cholesterol
sail-sale	fashionable festivals libraries semifinals
sea-see	teammates vegetarians
seen-scene	centipedes cleanliness
sent-cent-scent	centipedes destruction inspectors scientists
shear-sheer	cheerleaders
site-sight	exhausting
sore-soar	scoreboard skateboarding tournaments
stare-stair	caterpillars
steak-stake	breakthroughs
steal-steel	electricians elephants rattlesnakes rectangles
sum-some	mosquitoes
sun-son	astronauts dinosaurs pollutants unconscious
tail-tale	beautiful festivals triangles
tea-tee	literature teammates
their-there	kindhearted

tied-tide	accidents candidates outfielders
to-too-two	snowstorm
vain-vane-vein	anniversary carnivores vegetarians
we-wee	Milwaukee
weak-week	Milwaukee
wrap-rap	newspapers

■ Rimes, Spelling Patterns ■

ab	blizzards vocabulary
ace	Americans caterpillars perpendicular
ack*	blackbirds lumberjacks
ad	badminton blizzards
ade	endangered
aft	grandfathers
ag	magazines
age (page, passage)	breakthroughs geography grandfathers magazines skateboarding vegetarians
aid	blizzards dinosaurs
ail	Australia beautiful fashionable festivals libraries Philadelphia semifinals triangles
ain*	anniversary carnivores dinosaurs estimating gymnastics handicapped Minnesota pneumonia poinsettias skateboarding veterinarian
aint	fractions
air	caterpillars cauliflower
ait	skateboarding
ake*	breakthroughs Milwaukee rattlesnakes
ale*	beautiful fashionable festivals libraries Philadelphia semifinals triangles
all*	alligators calculators cauliflower footballs Philadelphia
am	amphibians immigrants
ame*	grandmothers Minnesota semifinals teammates
amp	champions

an*	amendments candidates fashionable fractions immigrants invitations pneumonia poinsettias vaccination
ance	accidents candidates
and	grandchildren thousands traditions
ane	anniversary carnivores estimating handicapped Minnesota pneumonia poinsettias
ang	subtracting
ange	grandfathers
ank*	kindhearted rattlesnakes skateboarding
ant	evaporation pollutants
ap*	amphibians carpenters champions newspapers perpendicular pneumonia spectacular
ape	carpenters geography
ar	Australia carnivores caterpillars
are	caterpillars cauliflower libraries
ark	blackbirds lumberjacks
art	astronauts barometers
ash*	amphibians characters fashionable mathematics
ask	skateboarding
ast	festivals footballs pollutants
at*	Australia badminton beautiful characters communication
atch	characters enthusiastic
ate*	beautiful carpenters celebrating decorations estimating evaporation exhausting rattlesnakes rectangles skateboarding teammates
ause	spectacular
ave	volcanoes
aw*	cauliflower newspapers
ax	relaxation
ay*	biography birthdays
aze	magazines

eak	breakthroughs Milwaukee rattlesnakes
eal	cheerleaders electricians elephants rattlesnakes relatives
eam	Americans mathematics teammates
ean	cleanliness electricians
eap	elephants
ear (hear, pear)	carelessness cauliflower cheerleaders newspapers
ease	carelessness cheerleaders
east	barometers festivals
eat*	amendments carpenters celebrating elephants literature rattlesnakes teammates
ed	candidates endangered wilderness
ee	interference literature refreshments reporters
eed	endangered independence
eek	Milwaukee
eel	cheerleaders electricians elephants rattlesnakes
een	electricians governments
eep	centipedes elephants telescopes
eer	cheerleaders
eet	elephants rattlesnakes
eight	frightening
elf	unsuccessful
ell*	bullfighter cauliflower millimeters volleyballs
elt	beautiful unemployment
en	amendments pneumonia
end	accidents adventurous independence presidents wilderness
ence	interference unpredictable
ense	centipedes cleanliness

ent	centipedes Connecticut continent destruction environment inspectors interception presidents refreshments scientists veterinarian
ess	carelessness misunderstood presidents responsible
est*	destruction interviews mathematics refreshments reporters scientists
et	carpenters estimating tournaments unemployment
ew	cauliflower
ice*	cleanliness continent crocodiles elections inspectors scientists
ick*	blackbirds ducklings mockingbirds
id	blackbirds blizzards
ide*	candidates neighborhood outfielders presidents
idge	neighborhood
ie	accidents literature
ief	frightening
ight*	bullfighter frightening Pittsburgh
ike	kilometers Milwaukee
ild	outfielders
ile	Baltimore millimeters outfielders semifinals
ilk	kilometers
ill*	alligators bullfighter cauliflower millimeters Philadelphia
im	immigrants
ime	kilometers millimeters
imp	champions
in*	contagious immigrants Minnesota pneumonia
inch	champions handicapped
ind	badminton neighborhood
ine*	frightening ingredients Minnesota pneumonia

ing*	contagious ducklings ingredients subtracting
ink*	ducklings kindhearted mockingbirds
ip*	amphibians champions comprehension handicapped
ir	Australia
ire	frightening interference interviews
ird	birthdays
irt	birthdays
ish	fashionable
ist	festivals
it*	Australia badminton estimating hibernation mosquitoes
itch	enthusiastic mathematics
ive (give, dive)	vegetarians
o	decorations interception invitations
oad	traditions
oak	skateboarding
oan	grandmothers relaxation
oar	hibernation scoreboard skateboarding
oast	antibiotics barometers fractions traditions
oat	antibiotics footballs
ob	vocabulary volleyballs
ock*	mockingbirds
ode	democracy
oil	Baltimore outfielders
oke*	bookstore kilometers skateboarding
old	outfielders
ole	cholesterol
oll	alligators calculators cholesterol pollutants
om	community
on	unconscious vaccination

one (done, bone)	Connecticut continent encouragement fashionable grandmothers hibernation Minnesota photosynthesis relaxation volcanoes
ong	governments
ook	bookstore
ool	cholesterol crocodiles footballs psychologist
oom	meteorologists
oon	snowstorm unconscious volcanoes
oop	hippopotamus psychologist
oost	bookstore
oot	bookstore hippopotamus meteorologists
op*	champions comprehension
ope	geography telescopes
ore*	Baltimore bookstore comprehension hibernation neighborhood rhinoceros scoreboard skateboarding
orn	carnivores fractions
ort	astronauts reporters
ose	crocodiles reporters
oss	misunderstood responsible telescopes
ost (cost, host)	cholesterol psychologist telescopes
ot*	congratulations continent nutrition precipitation thousands unfortunate
ote	continent environment
ough	breakthroughs greenhouse
ought	breakthroughs
ound	adventurous dinosaurs thousands underdogs
ount	communication community
our (our, four)	astronauts unsatisfactory
out	astronauts destruction hippopotamus nutrition pollutants thousands
outh	hippopotamus
ove	carnivores governments volcanoes

ow (how, show)	cauliflower snowstorm
oy	biography community democracy unemployment
ub	subtracting vocabulary
uck*	ducklings lumberjacks
ude	underdogs unpredictable
udge	underdogs
ue	breakthroughs measuring mosquitoes spectacular unsuccessful
ug*	greenhouse measuring
ull	bullfighter
um	multiplying
ump*	campgrounds hippopotamus multiplying
un	astronauts contagious undernourished unsuccessful
une	unfortunate
ung	contagious ducklings greenhouse subtracting
unk*	ducklings
urge	underdogs
urse	countries
urt	Pittsburgh
us	spectacular
use	unsuccessful outfielders spectacular
ush (bush, hush)	Pittsburgh toothbrushes
ust	astronauts countries Pittsburgh toothbrushes
ut	astronauts community nutrition thousands
ute	spectacular

■ Compound Words ■

airline	electricians
another	grandmothers
anteater	rattlesnakes
armrest	barometers grandmothers

blackbirds	blackbirds
cannot	vaccination
earring	grandchildren
footballs	footballs
freshmen	refreshments
grandchild	grandchildren
grandchildren	grandchildren
grandfathers	grandfathers
grandmothers	grandmothers
greenhouse	greenhouse
handouts	thousands
hothouse	toothbrushes
indoor	decorations
itself	festivals
kindhearted	kindhearted
legroom	meteorologists
mockingbirds	mockingbirds
newspapers	newspapers
outbreak	breakthroughs
outfield	outfielders
outfielders	outfielders
outrage	breakthroughs
outride	outfielders
outrun	unfortunate
outset	toothbrushes
outside	outfielders
overtime	environment
raincoat	unsatisfactory
rattlesnakes	rattlesnakes
redhead	kindhearted
sandbag	skateboarding
scoreboard	scoreboard
seesaw	newspapers
sidestep	presidents

skateboarding	skateboarding
snowstorm	snowstorm
softball	footballs
someone	comprehension
songbird	mockingbirds
stagehand	grandfathers
stepson	inspectors photosynthesis poinsettias
suitcase	enthusiastic
sunset	misunderstood
sunrise	misunderstood
teammates	teammates
teapot	poinsettias
tiptoe	photosynthesis poinsettias
toenails	sensational
toothbrushes	toothbrushes
turnout	unfortunate
underdogs	underdogs
upright	Pittsburgh
uptight	Pittsburgh

LETTER STRIPS

1	2	3	7	9	11	14	16	17	19	20	21
										t	
										s	
										r	
										r	t
	v	v					t			k	r
t	t	t	v	t	t	t	s	s	t	h	l
s	s	s	r	s	n	l	r	r	s	h	h
n	r	r	r	r	m	f	h	k	r	g	g
d	d	l	n	r	d	b	d	d	k	b	f
c	u	o	y	n	b	u	b	c	b	u	b
i	o	i	i	o	o	i	y	b	o	o	u
e	e	a	a	a	i	e	i	i	o	e	i
a	a	a	a	a	a	a	a	a	e	a	e

208

© 1997 Good Apple

LETTER STRIPS

Letter strips read top to bottom for each numbered column:

22	24	25	26	27	28	29	30	32	33	34	36
											t
	s			t						s	n
t	s	v	t	r	w	r	t			r	n
r	s	s	r	r	r	l	n	s	r	l	m
l	n	r	n	p	p	g	d	p	s	h	c
c	r	o	p	l	f	b	n	r	h	d	c
u	c	i	c	i	u	i	c	h	d	h	o
o	e	o	e	i	o	i	i	c	e	o	o
a	e	i	e	e	i	o	e	e	e	o	i
a	a	a	a	a	a	a	e	a	a	e	a

© 1997 Good Apple

22 24 25 26 27 28 29 30 32 33 34 36

209

38	39	39	41	42	43	44	45	47	48	49	50
	t										
r	s										
p	n										
n	n						r	t			
m	l		t			s	s	t			
h	g		s	t	t	r	r	r	s	s	t
c	g		n	n	n	c	r	d	r	k	s
o	u		u	n	c	c	c	d	n	g	l
o	o		u	n	c	o	o	u	d	k	c
i	o		o	c	o	o	o	u	u	o	o
e	i		i	i	i	i	i	e	o	u	i
e	a		i	i	i	i	i	e	o	u	e
e	a	t	a	e	e	e	a	e	a	i	e

51	52	54	55	56	57	59	60	61	62	63	64
			t								
t	s	t	v	t	v	s			t	t	
r	t	s	t	n	t	u			r	n	r
n	p	s	n	n	n	n	v	t	n	h	p
c	h	h	m	g	p	p	f	s	l	g	g
i	l	u	o	g	o	o	s	f	f	g	g
i	h	i	o	i	o	o	f	b	c	f	h
e	e	i	i	i	e	i	b	b	o	i	y
e	e	e	e	e	a	e	o	o	i	i	e
a	a	a	e	a	a	a	a	a	a	e	a

LETTER STRIPS

65	66	67	68	69	70	73	75	76	77	79
	r									
v	r	t					t			t
t	n	s	t			t	s	u	t	r
s	n	r	s	r		s	p	n	t	u
r	l	n	r	s	t	p	p	d	s	r
n	h	h	n	n	n	m	m	n	s	r
n	g	g	m	h	s	u	c	n	r	n
m	d	f	h	g	m	h	i	g	n	f
g	c	d	d	u	g	o	c	d	p	i
o	i	e	o	o	y	o	e	i	c	e
e	e	a	o	e	i	a	e	i	o	e
e	a	a	a	e	a	a	e	e	e	e

212

© 1997 Good Apple

LETTER STRIPS

80	83	84	85	86	87	88	89	90	91	94	95
								t			
								s		t	
								s		s	s
	t			s		t		r	t	s	r
w	r		t	r	t	t	s	m	s	n	n
v	n	s	t	m	z	s	r	l	r	r	g
t	h	r	r	j	m	m	r	g	m	n	k
s	d	r	r	k	n	h	n	l	m	d	g
r	d	b	u	j	m	c	m	o	l	u	d
n	i	i	i	b	g	i	g	o	l	o	c
i	i	i	i	u	i	i	u	o	i	o	b
i	e	i	e	e	i	e	e	i	i	i	o
e	e	e	e	e	a	a	a	e	e	e	i
e	a	a	a	a	a	a	a	e	e	e	i

LETTER STRIPS

96	97	99	100	101	102	103	105	109	110	111	112
							t				
						r	s			t	
		h	r				p	s		t	s
	t	h	n		t		p	s	t	r	t
s	p	g	w	t	r	n	s	t	p	s	s
s	n	h	s	r	s	r	p	n	s	r	p
q	m	d	r	r	t	l	n	p	c	s	l
m	l	b	p	t	n	f	d	c	o	n	h
u	g	o	p	r	d	u	c	h	i	r	g
o	y	o	n	n	u	i	y	n	o	n	c
i	u	o	n	u	i	i	o	l	i	d	y
i	i	i	e	i	o	e	i	u	o	i	o
e	i	e	a	i	e	a	e	a	a	e	i

214

LETTER STRIPS

113	114	115	116	117	118	119	120	121	122	124	125
											t
		s							s	r	s
	t	s							r	t	r
t	s	r				s	s	t	d	s	n
s	r	n	v	x	s	s	r	s	c	n	k
r	n	m	t	t	t	r	p	n	b	l	g
n	g	h	s	r	r	n	n	h	o	o	d
k	c	f	r	o	l	l	b	c	i	i	b
e	e	e	i	i	p	o	o	o	o	o	i
a	a	e	e	a	e	e	i	i	e	e	e
a	a	e	a	a	e	e	e	e	a	a	a

126	127	128	129	130	131	132	133	134	135	136	137
						t					
		t				t	t	t		s	s
w	s	t	t	t	t	s	t	r	s	s	r
t	r	r	t	s	s	s	r	n	r	n	n
s	c	g	s	p	p	h	h	m	l	n	g
r	c	c	m	l	d	n	b	u	d	c	d
n	u	b	e	o	u	u	u	o	o	u	u
m	e	u	e	e	o	o	o	o	i	o	o
o	a	i	a	e	o	o	o	e	i	o	o
o	a	a	a	e	a	e	a	a	a	i	e

LETTER STRIPS

138	139	140	141	142	143	145	146	148	149	150
s				t					v	
r	t			t					v	
n	p		t	s	s			v	s	
n	m	t	p	s	s		v	t	v	
h	m	n	p	n	s	s	v	n	n	w
d	l	n	n	f	n	s	r	r	s	s
u	y	f	d	y	c	f	s	n	c	l
o	u	u	b	u	c	f	l	g	b	y
i	o	o	i	o	u	i	c	i	o	o
e	e	a	i	a	u	i	i	i	e	i
e	e	a	e	a	e	e	e	a	a	e

217

LETTER STRIPS

4	5	6	8	10	12	13	15	18	23	31	35
											s
t	s	s	t			t			t	s	s
n	r	p	n	s	t	r	r	z	n	p	n
u	r	n	c	u	s	s	h	s	d	u	n
m	m	h	b	r	m	m	g	r	d	m	l
m	c	b	o	u	l	b	b	l	c	m	c
d	i	i	o	u	i	o	y	d	i	h	i
e	e	i	i	a	i	o	o	b	e	o	e
e	a	a	i	a	a	e	e	i	a	o	e
a	a	a	a	a	a	a	a	a	a	a	a

219

LETTER STRIPS

35	31	23	18	15	13	12	10	8	6	5	4
S								T			
S	P	T			T		T	S	S	S	T
N	N	N	Z	R	R	R	S	N	N	R	N
L	M	D	R	P	M	M	L	C	M	N	M
C	H	C	L	H	B	L	U	B	H	C	M
I	C	I	D	G	O	O	A	O	B	I	D
E	O	E	B	B	E	I	I	I	I	I	E
A	A	A	I	Y	O	E	A	I	I	E	E
A	A	A	D	O	E	O	A	O	B	C	D
A	A	A	I	I	A	I	A	I	I	I	M
A	A	A	A	A	A	A	A	A	A	A	M
A	A	A	A	A	A	A	A	A	A	A	A
A	A	A	A	A	A	A	A	A	A	A	A

© 1997 Good Apple

220

LETTER STRIPS

37	40	46	53	58	71	72	74	78	81	82	92
	t					t		t		t	
t	t	r		x	p	r	t	t	v	s	w
n	n	m	n	s	p	n	s	r	p	r	m
m	c	d	g	n	h	m	r	n	s	m	l
c	c	c	d	h	d	b	m	c	n	l	k
y	u	c	d	g	c	o	g	o	o	k	u
u	o	y	i	u	i	i	i	i	i	o	i
o	i	e	e	e	i	e	e	i	i	i	e
i	e	a	a	a	a	a	a	e	a	e	a

221

LETTER STRIPS

	T		T			P				T	
W	S	V	T	T	T	P			R	T	T
M	R	T	R	S	R	H	X	R	M	N	N
L	M	T	P	R	N	D	T	N	D	N	M
K	L	S	N	N	H	D	S	G	C	C	M
U	K	N	C	M	B	C	H	D	C	C	C
I	O	N	O	M	O	I	G	D	Y	U	Y
E	I	I	I	G	I	E	U	E	O	O	U
E	E	I	E	I	E	A	E	E	E	I	O
A	E	A	E	A	A	A	A	A	A	E	I
92	**82**	**81**	**78**	**74**	**72**	**71**	**58**	**53**	**46**	**40**	**37**

222

Letter strips (read bottom-to-top):

93	98	104	106	107	108	123	144	147			
											k
											j
		p			t		v			h	z
		l	t		s	s	t	v	d	g	x
t	t	h	r	p	s	n	n	r	c	f	w
s	s	h	p	n	s	m	c	l	b	d	v
n	r	d	h	m	p	l	c	r	b	d	t
m	y	i	g	u	o	f	o	y	u	c	s
i	i	i	b	o	n	i	i	o	y	b	r
e	e	a	u	e	e	e	a	a	o	u	q
a	e	a	i	a	a	a	a	a	a	i	p
										a	n
											m
											l

LETTER STRIPS

		147	144	123	108	107	106	104	98	93
			J			V		T		P
	Z	K	H		T	S		S		P
	X	D	G	V	S	S	T	N	T	L
	W	C	F	R	N	N	S	P	S	H
	V	B	D	C	M	N	S	R	R	D
	T	Y	C	C	L	O	U	H	M	N
	S	U	B	O	F	I	N	G	Y	O
	R	O	Y	I	I	O	M	B	I	I
	Q	I	U	A	E	E	U	I	E	E
	P	E	O	A	A	I	O	U	A	E
	N	A	A	A	A	E	O	B	A	I
	M		A			A		G	E	O
	L									A

© 1997 Good Apple

224